S. HRG. 104—97

THE EMPLOYMENT SITUATION

HEARINGS

BEFORE THE

JOINT ECONOMIC COMMITTEE
CONGRESS OF THE UNITED STATES

ONE HUNDRED FOURTH CONGRESS

FIRST SESSION

JANUARY 6, 1995

Printed for the use of the Joint Economic Committee

U.S. GOVERNMENT PRINTING OFFICE
92-610 CC WASHINGTON: 1995

For sale by the U.S. Government Printing Office
Superintendent of Documents, Congressional Sales Office, Washington, DC 20402
ISBN 0-16-047514-7

JOINT ECONOMIC COMMITTEE

[Created pursuant to Sec. 5(a) of Public Law 304, 79th Congress]

SENATE

CONNIE MACK, Florida,
Chairman
WILLIAM V. ROTH, JR., Delaware
LARRY E. CRAIG, Idaho
ROBERT F. BENNETT, Utah
RICK SANTORUM, Pennsylvania
ROD GRAMS, Minnesota
JEFF BINGAMAN, New Mexico
PAUL S. SARBANES, Maryland
EDWARD M. KENNEDY, Massachusetts
CHARLES S. ROBB, Virginia

HOUSE OF REPRESENTATIVES

JIM SAXTON, New Jersey,
Vice Chairman
THOMAS W. EWING, Illinois
JACK QUINN, New York
DONALD A. MANZULLO, Illinois
MARK SANFORD, South Carolina
MAC THORNBERRY, Texas
FORTNEY PETE STARK, California
DAVID R. OBEY, Wisconsin
LEE H. HAMILTON, Indiana
KWEISI MFUME, Maryland

ROBERT N. MOTTICE, *Executive Director*
JAMES LEE PRICE, *Minority Staff Director*

Contents

Opening Statements of Members

Witness

Submissions For The Record

THE DECEMBER EMPLOYMENT SITUATION

Friday, January 6, 1995

CONGRESS OF THE UNITED STATES,
JOINT ECONOMIC COMMITTEE,
WASHINGTON, D.C.

The Committee met at 9:30 a.m., in Room SD-430 of the Dirksen Senate Office Building, the Honorable Connie Mack, Chairman of the Committee, presiding.

Present: Senators Mack and Sarbanes, Representatives Saxton, Hamilton, Wyden and Manzullo.

OPENING STATEMENT OF SENATOR CONNIE MACK, CHAIRMAN

Senator Mack. First of all, let me welcome everyone and indicate that it will be my effort to try to get these meetings started on time.

I am happy to welcome everyone to the first meeting of the Joint Economic Committee (JEC) under full Republican control in 40 years. Needless to say, this is a novel experience for all of us and one, I must say, Ron, I'm really pleased to have the opportunity to participate in.

As some of you may know, the Joint Economic Committee was established soon after World War II to provide economic analysis to the Congress as a foundation for fiscal policy. Throughout most of the nearly five decades, that analysis has supported a major role for the government in the economy.

Under the leadership of Vice Chairman Saxton and myself, this will change. My conviction is that wealth and prosperity emerge from the spirit of creativity that resides within individuals, not governments. This creativity is enhanced by policies of less taxes, less spending, less government and more freedom. These will be the watchwords of the JEC during the 104th Congress.

During the first 100 days, my hope is that the JEC will play an important role in helping to pass the Republican economic plan. It is critical that this plan be enacted because it is good for Americans, and the economy will reflect it. Americans want a balanced budget amendment. They want major tax cuts, major spending cuts, regulatory reform. They want the President to have a line-item veto. They want welfare reform. Americans want the Republican economic plan because they know that it will make their economic future much brighter.

As for today's hearings, it is a pleasure to welcome Commissioner Katharine Abraham, and we look forward to your unemployment report for December.

I think I can speak for the majority of this panel in saying that we have tremendous respect for the independence and statistical integrity of the Bureau of Labor Statistics (BLS) and in the high standards established by former Commissioner Janet Norwood.

I would encourage you to continue to maintain the independence of the BLS and its data from political forces. If you or anyone else at BLS ever need our help in this regard, please let us know. And I think that, again, I really speak for both sides of the aisle on that issue.

I'm delighted with much of what is in today's unemployment report. Two hundred fifty-six thousand more Americans at work in December, a drop in the unemployment rate to 5.4 percent, and an increase in manufacturing jobs is decidedly good news. Yet, this good news is bittersweet. Despite the fact that more Americans are working, their standards of living are falling.

Even though the economy is still growing, the fact is that this recovery continues to be hollow. Real median incomes of U. S. workers and their families, America's middle class, have declined over the past two years.

This gap between job growth and actual incomes is due in large part to high-tax, big government policies the economy is saddled with. As always, the unintended consequences of taxation and regulation are lower incomes and fewer opportunities for the middle class.

The unemployment data released this morning do not change this picture. The middle class feels it's trapped in what I call a "treadmill economy."

The latest available Census data for 1993 show that real median earnings for both male and female workers actually declined in 1993. BLS data has also shown that real median weekly earnings declined between the third quarters of 1993 and 1994. These are not the results one would expect from an economy in which job quality was rising. This, in turn, raises questions about the quality of the jobs that are being produced, and even the Clinton Administration now concedes that the middle class has not benefited from the economic growth that is reflected in the GDP numbers.

I imagine that my Democratic colleagues will say that the slowdown in job growth would be a direct result of the Federal Reserve policy -- that the Fed is choking the economy. But I would argue that the real culprit behind those figures is big government and the legacy of high-tax policies.

High taxes and hyper-regulation always bring an economy to its knees. Using the Fed to paper over these problems is a recipe for disaster. That is why revamping the Humphrey-Hawkins Act is high on my list of priorities.

This brings me to the Republican economic plan and why today's unemployment report is more evidence of why this plan must be enacted quickly.

Lower taxes, spending cuts, regulatory reform, elimination of unfunded mandates, and welfare reform are a recipe for prosperity. Our agenda will get the American people off the treadmill and the economy into the fast lane.

Congressman Wyden, I will turn to you and ask you if you have an opening statement you'd like to make.

[The prepared statement of Senator Mack appears in the Submissions for the Record.]

OPENING STATEMENT OF REPRESENTATIVE RON WYDEN

Representative Wyden. I do, Mr. Chairman. Let me start first by welcoming you and also extending my congratulations to you, Chairman Mack. I've enjoyed working with you since our days in the House, Connie. I think you are going to conduct the affairs of this Committee in a fair way, as has been the tradition.

I look forward, along with the other Democrats, in working closely with you and my friend from the House side as well.

Let me, if I might, just make a couple of comments with respect to the economic picture today.

First, I think that the country should take special note of the fact that wage growth continues to be moderate, something like 2.7 percent over the last few months. This should send a very powerful message, in particular to the Federal Reserve, with respect to the need for their holding the line on additional hikes in interest rates.

We all know that these interest rate hikes can be crippling to our economy, particularly to the small businesses of the country which are so important to our economic future. And certainly, the evidence that we now have that wage growth continues to be moderate, suggests a new reality with respect to the inflation situation, that wage growth does suggest that we are dealing with inflationary pressures in a realist way, and it ought to send a message to Dr. Greenspan that he should be very careful with respect to further interest rate hikes, and I think that wage growth makes the case for moderation with respect to any interest rate hikes.

I think also we ought to take note of the fact that the job picture has been bright over the last few months, 700,000 jobs in the last couple of months, 3.5 million in the last year.

I share your view, Mr. Chairman, that we need more better wage jobs, and I think that this is something that can be tackled in a bipartisan way. And it seems to me that what we need to do is to look particularly at how to target tax cuts towards reinvestment and reinvestment in job creation.

For example, I was one of the Democrats who voted for George Bush's capital gains tax cut. We know that that has been a source of considerable friction between the political parties.

Well, I have a new capital gains alternative which would tie tax cuts to reinvestment. And what I will be proposing is that we look at capital gains and we look at business tax cuts much like we do home ownership.

As you know, what happens with respect to home ownership, if the Mack family sells their house and takes the proceeds and reinvests in another house, because we have deemed home ownership important, we will say that the tax man will not cometh and the reinvestment in a new home go forward.

I will be proposing the same thing for the capital gains issue. If a small business is sold and the owner is willing to take a portion of those proceeds and reinvest them in another small business, thereby keeping the dollars in the productive job-producing sector of the economy, then I think that that should be recognized as a stimulus to entrepreneurship and small business.

I've been getting good reactions from both sides of the aisle to this kind of approach with respect to capital gains. I think this is the kind of idea we ought to explore on a bipartisan basis.

And again, Chairman Mack, on behalf of the Democrats, we welcome you. We have appreciated your fairness in the past and look forward to working with you.

Senator Mack. Thank you. I appreciate your comments and look forward to working with you as well. And I also want to welcome Congressman Manzullo, who I guess technically has not been appointed to the Committee as of yet, but we're delighted that you're here and we'd ask you if you'd like to make an opening comment.

OPENING STATEMENT OF REPRESENTATIVE DONALD MANZULLO

Representative Manzullo. Well, first of all, it's a great honor to be here, Senator Mack. I find it particularly interesting that Mr. Wyden is on the Committee. Ron and I worked on two different ends of trying to expand trade opportunities in the area of communications and computers. I think yours got through. Mine got stalled in the rewrite of The Export Administration Act.

But I'm very much interested in what we can do in this country to try to spur economic growth in the area of exports because jobs involving exports pay on the average, 17 percent more than jobs not involved in exports. And about 70 to 80 percent of the growth in the real high paying jobs in the past five or six years has been in those areas involved in exports.

I'm also delighted that a former Chairman of the House Foreign Affairs Committee, still Ranking on Foreign Affairs, Mr. Hamilton, is here and we can discuss many of these issues involving economics with regard to our areas of exports and imports.

So it's a real job to be here. I look forward to the testimony of the witnesses.

Senator Mack. Thank you.

Congressman Hamilton, let me welcome you.

OPENING STATEMENT OF REPRESENTATIVE LEE HAMILTON

Representative Hamilton. Going through opening statements?

Senator Mack, let me just say congratulations to you as you take the Chairmanship of this Committee. We look forward to working with you and we look forward to your leadership.

Nice to be with Mr. Manzullo on another committee. Thank you.

Senator Mack. We're delighted that you're here. I have nothing but the greatest regard for you and I'm delighted that you're on the Committee with us.

Representative Hamilton. Thank you.

Senator Mack. Commissioner, now we will turn to you and ask you for your report.

STATEMENT OF THE HONORABLE KATHARINE G. ABRAHAM, COMMISSIONER, BUREAU OF LABOR STATISTICS

ACCOMPANIED BY THOMAS PLEWES, ASSOCIATE COMMISSIONER, EMPLOYMENT AND UNEMPLOYMENT STATISTICS, AND KENNETH V. DALTON, ASSOCIATE COMMISSIONER, PRICES AND LIVING CONDITIONS

Ms. Abraham. Thank you very much, Mr. Chairman, members of the Committee.

I, as always, appreciate the opportunity to be here to comment on labor market data that we released earlier this morning.

The December data released today sustained the pattern of labor market improvements that was fairly pervasive throughout 1994. Payroll employment continued to advance, increasing, as you noted, by 256,000 over the month. Unemployment remained on its downward trend at 5.4 percent. The unemployment rate was 1.3 percentage points below its level at the beginning of 1994.

December's gain in employment, as measured by our survey of businesses, brings the increase in payroll employment for all of 1994 to 3.5 million. This exceeded the prior year's gain by over a million and was the largest in the past decade.

Factory employment, which you also commented upon, rose by 54,000 in December, with gains widespread throughout the individual manufacturing industries. The largest increases occurred in fabricated metals and electronic equipment.

Manufacturing job growth totaled nearly 300,000 for the year as a whole, compared with a loss of 130,000 in 1993. The extraordinary high levels of weekly hours and also of factory overtime during 1994 provide additional evidence of the strength in the demand for labor in the manufacturing sector.

Although construction employment showed little movement in December, for all of 1994, employment in the industry rose by about 300,000, the largest annual gain in 10 years.

The services industry added 110,000 jobs in December, with increases in business, health, and social services. Over the year, employment growth in services totaled 1.6 million.

Retail trade also had substantial employment gains both in December -- 91,000 -- and over the year -- nearly 800,000. Most of December's gain was in eating and drinking places, which appear to have had a strong holiday season.

Holiday-related increases in package delivery and traveling lie behind the December employment increase in the transportation industry, and holiday-related shipping also contributed to an over-the-month gain in Federal Government postal employment.

Over the year, however, the number of Federal jobs has declined by about 50,000, and would have declined even more had the Postal Service been excluded from the figures.

Local governments, excluding education, shed 57,000 jobs in December. The main reason for that is that workers who had been brought on for the November elections were no longer on the payrolls in December.

I think this is worth noting, particularly because, absent the inclusion of the temporary election positions in the November job count, the December employment increase would have been larger and that for November correspondingly somewhat smaller.

So if you just take the raw figures, we had a big drop in employment growth, from 488,000 in November to 256,000 in December; adjusting the figures, the two months would have looked less different.

As is our normal practice at the end of the year, the seasonally adjusted estimates from the household survey have been revised to reflect updated seasonal factors. Because of the major redesign of the household survey that was implemented in January, 1994, this year we have revised only the data for the last 12 months.

Like the estimates from the employers survey, the data from the household survey show substantial improvement in the labor market during 1994.

As I mentioned earlier, the unemployment rate over the year from January through December dropped 1.3 percentage points, from 6.7 percent in January to 5.4 percent in December. Jobless rates improved during the year for adults and for teenagers, for whites, for blacks, for Hispanics.

In addition, the number of persons working part-time when they would have preferred full-time work declined by nearly 650,000.

Since January, total employment has risen by 2.7 million, raising the proportion of the population with jobs to a very high 63 percent. The labor force rose by 1.1 million over the January to December period.

In summary, as you suggested in your opening comments, the labor market showed strength in December as it did throughout 1994. Employment, as measured by both of our monthly surveys, has increased substantially over the year and unemployment has fallen.

My colleagues, Mr. Plewes, our Associate Commissioner for Employment and Unemployment Statistics, and Mr. Dalton, our Associate Commissioner for Prices and Living Conditions, and I would be very happy to answer any questions that members of the Committee might have.

[The prepared statement of Commissioner Abraham together with the Employment Situation and press release appear in the Submissions for the Record.]

Senator Mack. Neither one has comments they'd like to make at this point?

Ms. Abraham. Not at this point.

Senator Mack. All right. Thank you.

Senator Sarbanes, welcome.

OPENING STATEMENT OF SENATOR PAUL SARBANES

Senator Sarbanes. Well, thank you very much, Mr. Chairman. I want to congratulate you on assuming the Chairmanship of the Committee. We look forward to your leadership. And I want to congratulate Congressman Saxton on becoming the Vice Chairman of the Committee.

This Committee has done a lot of good work over the years, and we look forward to its continuing functioning as a positive and constructive force.

Thank you very much.

Senator Mack. And Vice Chairman Saxton, do you have an opening comment you'd like to make?

OPENING STATEMENT OF REPRESENTATIVE JIM SAXTON, VICE CHAIRMAN

Representative Saxton. Mr. Chairman, I have an opening statement that I would ask unanimous consent be placed in the record.

Senator Mack. Without objection.

Representative Saxton. I would just say that I'm very pleased with the numbers that Dr. Abraham is here to report to us this morning. We appreciate your candor, as usual. And just to say that the speculation that I've heard in the last couple of hours from the media and from other places is that we may be in store for another round of interest rate increases, which I find kind of interesting in light of the fact that the economy is apparently continuing to grow.

I think the question for all of us to ask ourselves, and perhaps each other, is what is it that's spurring the economy onward and upward and what is it that we as policymakers need to be mindful of in terms of monetary policy and other issues that are obviously very important aspects of this entire situation in which we find ourselves.

On the one hand, it seems to be very positive. On the other hand, no one wants higher interest rates on homes or automobiles or consumer goods.

Obviously, the Fed has an important role to play here, and we need to be mindful of what it is that we're going to see in the next month or two.

So thank you very much for being here, and we appreciate it.

[The prepared statement of Represenative Saxton appears in the Submisssions for the Record.]

Senator Mack. We will now proceed to questions. I think that we will allot five minutes. That way, I think it will move a little bit faster.

I'm going to begin in the area, frankly, that I would just as soon avoid, but I think it's important that we get out on the table.

You and I had a pretty good discussion yesterday again about the importance of the independence of the BLS, and obviously assured me of your commitment to that.

But yesterday, there was a story in *The Washington Post* -- that discussed a central oversight group down at the Labor Department that Secretary Reich has put together to respond to a Republican-controlled

Congress. And the implication would be that that group is politically motivated.

There was no, at least that I could see, statement of exemption of the BLS. Did you see the memo? Was it sent to you? Did anybody in your agency receive the memo?

Ms. Abraham. I did not receive a memo. I understand that such a group was formed.

The Deputy Commissioner at the Bureau of Labor Statistics, who is a career employee, is planning to attend the first meeting or meetings of this group to determine what exactly it is the group is to do and whether or not it would be appropriate for us to continue to participate.

It's not clear to me at this point what the function of this group would be.

Senator Mack. Do you have any concerns about the functions of that group?

Ms. Abraham. I guess I think that, to the extent that the Congress has interest in what's going on in the Department of Labor generally, there may be value in communication among the different parts of the department.

Beyond that, I'm not sure what our role in such a group would be.

Senator Mack. Well, then, let me be a little bit more plain, then. The concern is the independence of the BLS. Maybe I ought to ask you why it's important that there be independence because you were pretty clear about it yesterday, that you thought that that was pretty significant.

So rather than for me to say it, let me let you say it.

Ms. Abraham. Well, as you may know, the Bureau has a long history. I am the only person at the Bureau who is not a career employee, and historically, commissioners have often turned into career employees, although they are appointed to the position.

I guess I think that it's important that that be the case. I think it's important that the Bureau not become involved in policy discussions or political discussions in any way because our job is to provide data that everyone can rely upon. And if there were any question that anyone with a political or a policy interest were in a position to influence the numbers that we reported, which they are not, I think there would be questions about the usefulness of our data for information purposes, about their value to everyone who needs information to support decisions that they're making.

Senator Mack. Well, again, I appreciate that. You were very clear yesterday in your intentions to make sure that the integrity of the BLS is protected. And I'm quite sure that you will in fact do that.

As I commented in my opening statement, we will be of assistance to you, and on both sides of the aisle, I don't think there's any question. There's been a strong feeling about that year after year.

But I hope you can understand, without there being some statement from the Labor Department that your Agency, in essence, is being excluded from that kind of political activity, it behooves me to raise that.

I hope you can understand my concern with that. I guess I would ask you if you would let us know after your folks have attended that meeting, what your intentions are as to whether there will be a representative of your agency at those meetings in the future.

It looked like, from the information that we had, these meetings would take place probably once a week. I'd certainly have no problems with the Administration trying to prepare itself so that it can have dialogue with the Congress about what they have to say and how they want to defend it.

Ms. Abraham. I certainly would be happy to do that. I should hasten to add that there has been nothing that has happened in my time at the Bureau of Labor Statistics--and I could perhaps ask my colleagues to speak to this--no pressure of any sort, no actions of any kind on the part of the Department of Labor that were intended to or would have compromised the independence of the Bureau. The political leadership in the Department has been very cognizant and very respectful of the importance of maintaining that independence.

Senator Mack. And again, I recognize that. But I am responding again to the article that was in the paper that indicates that there may be a change.

I just want to make sure that you're aware of that potential. If you are of the impression after this first meeting that the primary purpose, or even an implied purpose, of the group is political in nature, would you make a commitment to this Committee that you will make every effort to see that the Secretary is informed and that you would inform him directly that your agency will not be participating in that activity?

Ms. Abraham. I certainly will do that, and would have done that in any event.

Senator Mack. Well, frankly, I would ask the Secretary to make a statement that would clarify and make it certain that those parts of the Labor Department that are involved in providing statistical data, which the Congress has to rely on, will not be part of that political effort.

Congressman Wyden?

Representative Wyden. Thank you, Mr. Chairman.

Dr. Abraham, it seems to me that the numbers that you're putting out now, in effect, are a brief for not raising interest rates again. These numbers with respect to inflation, I think are exceptional. I'd like to just explore this with you because you look at the moderation with respect to inflation and it is really exceptional.

The core rate of inflation is what really counts. And the core rate excludes food and energy. Why don't we begin by asking you what the core inflation rate has been so far this year?

Ms. Abraham. So far this year, the core rate of inflation, the Consumer Price Index for all items, less food and energy, has been running at 2.8 percent on an annualized basis.

Representative Wyden. My understanding is that the core inflation rate has also gone down over the last couple of years. It's gone down in '92 and then went down again in 1993.

Is that correct?

Ms. Abraham. Yes, that is correct. The core rate of inflation was 4.4 percent in 1991, 3.3 percent in 1992, 3.2 percent in 1993, and then, as I said already, has been running at an annualized rate through November of 2.8 percent this year.

In 1994. Not this year.

Representative Wyden. When was the last time the core inflation rate was this low, 2.8 percent?

Ms. Abraham. I have a table here that goes back to 1980 and there was no year between 1980 and the present when it was that low.

Ken, do you have figures going back farther?

Mr. Dalton. I'm afraid I don't have them. No, I don't.

Ms. Abraham. My guess is that it would have been sometime in the '60s, probably.

Representative Wyden. Is it correct to say that the core rate continues to fall? My understanding is it was 2.8 for the past 11 months and then it has fallen again most recently.

Ms. Abraham. I do not have month-by-month data in front of me here.

Representative Wyden. Does your evidence indicate that the core inflation rate essentially fell throughout 1994?

Ms. Abraham. I'm afraid all I have in front of me -- actually, let me pull something out here that should have this. What the chart I was looking at had in it was --

Representative Wyden. It certainly is down compared to 1993.

Ms. Abraham. It's certainly down compared to '93 and '92. If you want to ask another question, I'll keep looking for the month-by-month figures.

Mr. Dalton. At least since mid-year, it's been fairly stable.

Representative Wyden. If someone summarized 1994 this way, Dr. Abraham, that there was strong growth, low unemployment, and falling inflation, would the Department disagree with that summary?

Ms. Abraham. Without the month-to-month figures on inflation in front of me, I'm not in a very good position to answer that.

Do you have that?

Mr. Dalton. Characterizing the whole year --

Ms. Abraham. A period of falling inflation?

Mr. Dalton. Well, certainly the rate through the first 11 months is lower. It's actually the same as the total for last year. If you look at the core rate --

Representative Wyden. But in terms of an overall assessment of the year, I look at the economic growth figures that you've given us for '94. They're probably in the vicinity of 3.7, 3.8 percent on the growth issue.

I look at the unemployment figures that you've given us--about 5.6 percent was where we were in November, some change there... then that declining inflation consideration that I just explored with you with the rate of only 2.8 percent--

I look at 1994, particularly as Dr. Greenspan moves to consider further rate hikes, and I see strong growth, low unemployment, falling inflation.

And what I'd like to see is whether you all, who have to keep the books and measure this objectively, in any way disagree with that analysis.

92-610 - 95 - 2

Ms. Abraham. The facts, insofar as you're describing the facts that we just went through, those facts are accurate.

Representative Wyden. Okay. Let me ask one other question that deals with this matter you and I have discussed before.

Ms. Abraham. Yes.

Representative Wyden. I don't think the way you all keep the figures, and I think you do an admirable job with the tools that you have, really reflect this productivity revolution that we're seeing in our country with computers and software and technology.

You and I are exchanging letters on this point and I appreciate your candor on the issue. But what can be done to start getting better measures in areas where you admit we've got real problems, such as the service sector?

The letter that you most recently wrote me I thought was really alarming with respect to how little we are doing to accurately pick up on growth in the service sector and changes in the sector.

Maybe you could respond to that in my last question for this round.

Ms. Abraham. Well, there are a number of different measures that we put out and the answer I think is somewhat different, depending on what you're talking about.

With respect to the Producer Price Index, which is the measure of prices of goods sold by producers, coverage in the service sector is very low, as I noted in the letter that I sent you.

That's partly a resource issue, but it's partly also a conceptual issue, in that with a good such as a television set, it's pretty clear what you're pricing but when you talk about services that are being provided, it's less clear what you're pricing, and so there are some conceptual issues to be worked on as well in figuring out how to do that.

So I guess a very short answer is it's partly a resource issue, but it's also partly that there's some hard thinking that needs to be done.

Representative Wyden. Well, I will await the final response from the Department. But please understand how seriously I feel about this. There are issues about which the political parties clearly disagree.

One issue we won't disagree on, though, is that we are in the middle of a global productivity revolution that is technology-fueled and fueled by computers and software and the like. And I look sometimes at economic tools that you have and, as I say, I think you do an admirable job with what you have.

I kind of feel like we're riding into the next century in a model T with respect to economic measures.

I will await your final response. Maybe we can get into this a little more this morning. I thank you, Mr. Chairman. And, by the way, our friend from New Jersey was not here when I had a chance to throw some bouquets your way. But I also want to welcome the gentleman from New Jersey, Mr. Saxton.

We've worked together from Aging Committee days and he'll be very fair and very objective. I look forward to working with him.

Senator Mack. Thank you. At this time I will turn to the Vice Chairman and ask you to raise your questions.

Representative Saxton. Mr. Chairman, thank you very much.

Mr. Wyden has, I think, touched on really the central issue here. Obviously, we're all interested in making sure that the economy continues to do well, as the unemployment rate continues to drop, or at least stabilize itself at a very healthy rate.

The issue of inflation and how that relates to Fed activity is certainly one that is very central. Let me just ask some questions that relate to that to try to expand on the issue just a bit.

Dr. Abraham, Mr. Wyden's question that went to the core inflation rate and your response was, I believe, that the rate of inflation seems to be stable, that there doesn't seem to be any indication from a statistical point of view that there is any increase in the rate of inflation imminent, nor can you see anything in your statistical data that would indicate that we are looking at inflation in the foreseeable future.

Is that a fair statement?

Ms. Abraham. What we can tell you is that there is no indication in the data we have to date, which goes through November, of any acceleration in inflation.

Representative Saxton. Well --

Ms. Abraham. Actually, Ken can qualify that. Ken Dalton can add something.

Mr. Dalton. One qualification on that is that in the intermediate good component of the Producer Price Index, over the past several months, we have seen an accelerating rate of increase.

Now whether or not those price increases get passed on into final goods is a question we can't answer, but I think it's something that deserves some attention.

Ms. Abraham. Thank you for adding that.

Representative Saxton. Obviously, the Fed's concern is that they see this inflationary trend in underlying statistics and that would encourage the Fed to try to counter-act that by increasing interest rates.

Is that a fair statement, Mr. Dalton?

Mr. Dalton. Well, I certainly can't speak for the Fed. I can say what I've read in the newspapers. It would seem that they are concerned about future developments more so than past developments. And they are concerned about prices at earlier levels in the manufacturing or production process than are evident, for example, in the Consumer Price Index.

I think their view of the Consumer Price Index is that it is a lagging indicator, in some sense. And given their responsibilities, what they need is a leading indicator.

Representative Saxton. What kind of leading indicator, what would you look at in terms of leading indicators? What kind of statistical data do we have to look at?

Mr. Dalton. I can only look at my own, the information that I myself -- well, we -- produce.

Representative Saxton. Let me ask you a question. I know that oftentimes we ask questions that are difficult for you all to answer because when we stray very far from statistics, we become subjective.

But what is it about the economy or what is it about monetary policy that you think might be fueling these fears of inflation? And what is it that is driving the statistical data to fuel the concern of the Fed?

Ms. Abraham. As I guess Ken has indicated, we really are not in a position to speak to what they might be looking at.

Ken has already pointed to the one thing in our data that we can see that might be leading them to be concerned.

As you know, we don't have a crystal ball in terms of looking into the future and we very much try to stay out of making projections or anything of that sort.

So that's just really not something we are in a position to speak to.

Representative Saxton. Are you personally concerned about inflation currently? And if you were in a position to make decisions relative to monetary policy, do you think that continuing to tighten at this point is justified activity?

Ms. Abraham. That's just not something I've really thought about.

Representative Saxton. I thought that that might be your response.

(Laughter.)

Ms. Abraham. I thought you might.

(Laughter.)

Representative Saxton. Mr. Chairman, thank you very much.

Senator Mack. Congressman Hamilton?

Representative Hamilton. Thank you, Mr. Chairman.

I want to go back to Mr. Wyden's like of questioning, if I may. He pointed out the growth in inflation and in unemployment figures. I think he said that growth for 1994 was about 4 percent. Correct me if I'm wrong anywhere. That inflation was down to 2.7 or 2.8 percent and that unemployment has dropped down to 5.4 percent.

Now, if you just look at -- I know you deal with a mountain of economic statistics. But if you look at these three statistics -- growth, unemployment, and inflation -- for most of us who are not economists, these are the most important statistics, it seems to me. These are the ones that the politicians focus on. These are ones the average people focus on.

How long has it been since we've seen that good a performance in the American economy?

Ms. Abraham. Well, maybe I could break it up into --

Representative Hamilton. No, overall. I don't want it broken up. I want it overall.

Ms. Abraham. The problem with my answering the question the way you've posed it is that I don't know how to make a value judgment about what weight I should attach to each of these things.

Representative Hamilton. I'm not asking you to make a value judgment. I'm just asking you to tell me how long has it been in the American economy since you've seen that good a performance on the three major economic indicators?

Ms. Abraham. Well, in terms of employment growth, you have go back 10 years, but inflation was running higher then. So I think you'd probably have to go back again to the '60s before you had that combination of that kind of growth, that kind of unemployment rate, that kind of inflation, altogether.

Representative Hamilton. I think you have to go back to -- I think you're right -- 1963 to 1964, when the economy grew about 4.8

percent. Unemployment fell from 5.7 to 5.2 percent. And core inflation, from 1.6 to 1.2 percent.

When you say you have a 5.4 percent unemployment rate today, how many people does that mean are unemployed, don't have jobs?

Ms. Abraham. Let's see. There were about 7.2 million unemployed people in December, seasonally adjusted.

Representative Hamilton. And on the job growth figures that I want to go over a little bit with you, we had the largest increase in jobs -- I guess we're talking about nonfarm jobs here.

Ms. Abraham. Nonfarm payroll jobs.

Representative Hamilton. Since 1984, in 1994.

Is that correct?

Ms. Abraham. That is correct.

Representative Hamilton. And we created 3.1 million new jobs during 1994.

Correct?

Ms. Abraham. That sounds correct.

Representative Hamilton. That's about right? Now, we hear constantly -- well, first, let me ask you. How about private-sector jobs, public-sector jobs?

How does that break down there, that 3.1 million?

Ms. Abraham. It looks more like 3.4 million to me.

Representative Hamilton. Okay.

Ms. Abraham. On private-sector jobs -- over January to December or December to December?

Representative Hamilton. Well, 1994.

Ms. Abraham. In 1994, we added 3.2 million private sector jobs.

Representative Hamilton. All private sector. Now, do you look into the quality --

Ms. Abraham. Almost all -- if you're taking December to December, it was 3.5 million total jobs, 3.2 private.

Representative Hamilton. That's all right. Okay. And is there an increase in government jobs, too?

Ms. Abraham. Federal employment fell over the year. Total government employment, went up some, including state and local government.

Representative Hamilton. Federal Government employment fell how much in 1994?

Ms. Abraham. Federal Government employment fell by 50,000. That Federal Government figure that I'm giving you includes the Postal Service. Postal Service employment was up some, so Federal employment otherwise would have been down more.

Representative Hamilton. But overall, government employment went up because state and local employment went up more than the Federal Government cut.

Is that it?

Ms. Abraham. That is correct. Overall, government employment, including state and local, was up 247,000.

Representative Hamilton. Quite an increase in state and local government jobs.

Okay. Now on these jobs that are created in the private sector, we hear a lot about lower paying jobs. Can you give me any indication of the quality of the jobs that were created?

Ms. Abraham. I can tell you some things about the kind of jobs that were created. More accurately, I can tell you some things about what kinds of jobs we added on net.

What I can tell you about is the industries in which we were adding jobs. We added 3.5 million payroll jobs altogether over the period from December, '93 through December, '94.

Representative Hamilton. Let me back up. I want to get you out of those statistics a little bit and just kind of get an overall impression.

Are we creating good paying jobs, or are most of these jobs that we're creating, the hamburger-flipping jobs?

Ms. Abraham. Taking a somewhat longer time perspective, and I see the continuation of a similar pattern in the past year, we've been creating jobs in industries that are somewhat lower paying, in occupations that are better paying.

So we're creating managerial-professional jobs disproportionately in service-providing industries. That's a very broad categorization of what we're doing.

It would not be an accurate characterization to say that we're primarily creating hamburger-flipping jobs.

Representative Hamilton. Thank you, Mr. Chairman.

Senator Mack. Congressman Manzullo?

Representative Manzullo. Thank you, Senator. I've got a comment and then a question.

I'm very much disturbed over a revelation that I saw in the newspaper a couple of days ago where Congressman Jim Moran has been fighting with the EPA, which has terminated contracts with the private sector, and then turned right around and hired employees of that private sector as official government employees.

I think something like 800 or 900 employees are in the process of being hired by the Federal Government.

Do you know of any other instances such as that, Dr. Abraham?

Ms. Abraham. I do not.

Representative Manzullo. Are there details of what's happened with that situation with the EPA?

Ms. Abraham. I don't know what the details of that situation are. I am not sure that we have anything in our statistics that would shed light directly on that, since even if we knew what was happening with Federal employment, we wouldn't know from our data what was happening to the number of contractors on board, I don't believe.

Is that correct, Tom?

Mr. Plewes. We don't have that information for the contractors that work for the Federal Government.

We do know that there's an increase still in contractors and contractor employment in the business services sector has grown fairly substantially. And we know that there's been a decline in the Federal Government.

I'm not sure if we have any proof of this kind of switch as you're talking about now.

Representative Manzullo. The question that I have, it's unrelated to this, but it deals with the American family earning more dollars, but taking home less in terms of the average median income.

What figures, if any, do you have to demonstrate the trend?

Ms. Abraham. Well, unfortunately, in terms of talking about what has happened to either median incomes or to median weekly earnings in a definitive way, we are handicapped by the fact that the Current Population Survey, which is the survey where those numbers come from, was revamped effective in January.

The survey had been a paper and pencil instrument. It was computerized, and the questions about earnings were modified.

I think that's an issue because I am not 100 percent confident in my own mind that the figures that we have for 1993 on income or the figures that we have on weekly earnings for 1994, are totally comparable with figures for earlier years.

That said, I can tell you what the figures show.

Representative Manzullo. What do we have?

Ms. Abraham. For what they're worth, and I think you have to be a little skeptical about drawing conclusions about the trend--

Representative Manzullo. We're all skeptical as to any figures. The question is that --

Ms. Abraham. I would hope that you're not generally skeptical about our figures.

(Laughter.)

Representative Manzullo. It could be a built-in institutional flaw in both Bodies.

Very simply, the question is that Americans are working more, but taking home less. I just wanted to see what figures you had on that, if any.

Ms. Abraham. I guess the most relevant figures that I have are probably the figures on median usual weekly earnings of full-time wage and salary workers.

Representative Manzullo. Which is?

Ms. Abraham. In constant dollars, that is, adjusted for inflation, our figures for the third quarter of 1994 show median weekly earnings for full-time wage and salary workers of $300 compared with the corresponding figure for the third quarter of 1993, $307.

But, as I said, I would be reluctant to conclude from that that there has indeed been a trend, given the changes in the survey that produces the figures.

Representative Manzullo. Are those figures adjusted for inflation?

Ms. Abraham. Yes, they are.

Representative Manzullo. So if those figures are correct, and I appreciate your candor and skepticism of them, we went from $307 to $300, and if inflation was 3 percent, that's actually four less dollars.

Ms. Abraham. Seven less dollars. These were already adjusted for inflation.

Representative Manzullo. I'm sorry. Seven less dollars.

Ms. Abraham. Seven less dollars.

Representative Manzullo. That's correct.

Ms. Abraham. Right.

Senator Mack. Thank you. Congressman Wyden?

Representative Wyden. Just one additional question for purposes of the long term, and I think Chairman Mack is interested in a lot of these issues, and I am as well.

The Contract With America, and a number of the Republican proposals talk about a change in the regulatory process, particularly looking at ways to make regulations less burdensome and less intrusive on business.

It's a view I share and one where I think some very good bipartisan work can be accomplished because there's no question that I hear it from my small businesses constantly that a lot of our small businesses are just drowning in paperwork, regulatory hassles, and the like.

There is one issue that the Republicans have raised in the Contract With America and elsewhere that I am interested in, even methodologically, how you would get into it. And that is that under the regulatory proposals they are discussing, they're talking about a cost/benefit analysis that would require placing a cost, so-called, on human life.

As I look at it, I don't see where the Federal Government is going to go to really get this kind of data.

Now, my understanding is that you all keep track of data with respect to work place injuries and illnesses.

Is that correct?

Ms. Abraham. That is correct.

Representative Wyden. Do you think that you could take this data and objectively use it so as to be able to place a cost, so-called, on human life in the context of a regulatory reform proposal?

Ms. Abraham. I would not know how to do that. I also would not think that that would ordinarily be the kind of job that would be assigned to the Bureau of Labor Statistics, since it's not something we could directly measure.

Representative Wyden. The irony is that this is the most accurate data that we've got, as far as I can tell. The Bureau does report the number of work days lost because of illness or injury.

Is that correct?

Ms. Abraham. The Bureau reports information on the number of people who suffered work place injuries or illnesses and then information on the distribution of how long they were out of work.

We do not produce a measure of total days lost.

Representative Wyden. Because my reading of your reports and your analysis, they're the most thorough in government. I don't know of anybody else who's doing them. And if you're saying that it's hard to take this data and use it for purposes of putting a so-called cost on human life, I don't know where somebody's going to go to get the data for that kind of regulatory approach.

Do you?

Ms. Abraham. I don't know, but I also have not thought about how you might approach that.

Representative Wyden. Well, we may want to talk about this further because -- well, let me ask you one other one.

The Bureau does not now report the economic cost of injuries and sicknesses or even death, do you?

Ms. Abraham. No, we do not. We report figures on numbers of injuries, numbers of deaths.

Representative Wyden. Would you be in a position, in your view, to even give an economic cost of injuries and illnesses now?

Ms. Abraham. Well, you would need a couple of pieces of information that we don't have at this point.

With respect to injuries, you would need some information on how long people who are injured, even those who were most seriously injured ultimately, ended up staying out of work, if that was the route you wanted to go.

We don't collect that information because we get our information from an annual survey that's conducted soon after the end of the year. And for the people who are most seriously injured, it's not yet known how long they're going to be out of work.

So it would have to be something done in more of a research mode, through studies that followed up on these people over the longer term.

Then you would also have to attach some dollar figure to each day that they were out of work. And that would really be beyond our purview, I suspect.

Representative Wyden. And you do think that it would be very difficult for you as an Agency to get into this question of, in effect, placing the so-called cost on human life as part of the regulatory process with the data you now have.

Ms. Abraham. Put that way, yes. I guess if what you wanted to talk about was the amount of forgone earnings that they had, there would be estimates that we probably could produce, if we collected additional information, on the lost earnings of those people who were injured.

We do not have that information at this time.

Representative Wyden. Mr. Chairman, I only bring this up by way of saying that, from this side, and speaking specifically for this member, I'm anxious to work with you and our colleagues to try to make the regulatory burden less on business, particularly small business.

But I would hope that, in some of these areas, such as placing a so-called cost on human life, there would be an effort to proceed very cautiously because I think that what we've heard from Dr. Abraham that this is an area that is going to be pretty difficult to calculate, even in terms of objective kind of data.

I would like to see a bipartisan effort to try to make the regulatory process work better, make it less burdensome, make it less cumbersome, particularly for small business.

I just fear getting involved in these questions of putting a so-called cost on human life as ones that are going to be problematic, let us say, at best, and I think literally impossible to do.

I thank you for the extra round.

Senator Mack. Senator Sarbanes?

Senator Sarbanes. Thank you very much, Mr. Chairman.

Commissioner, I'd like to just kind of establish some benchmarks here off the basis of the figures that you brought this morning.

As I understand it, you've reported now that the unemployment rate has declined now to 5.4 percent.

Is that correct?

Ms. Abraham. That is correct.

Senator Sarbanes. What was it at the beginning of the year, in January? 6.7?

Ms. Abraham. 6.7 percent.

Senator Sarbanes. Now when was the unemployment rate last as low as 5.4 percent?

Ms. Abraham. As you well know, our survey was redesigned in January, so the new figures and the old figures are not strictly comparable.

But bearing that in mind, the last time that the unemployment rate was as low as 5.4 percent was July of 1990.

Senator Sarbanes. All right. So it's July of 1990?

Ms. Abraham. That's correct.

Senator Sarbanes. So it's the best we've had in four-and-a-half years.

Ms. Abraham. That's correct, comparing the numbers, though they're not strictly comparable.

Senator Sarbanes. Right. Now, how many jobs were added to nonfarm payrolls in 1994?

Ms. Abraham. Between December of '93 and December of '94, nonfarm payrolls rose by 3.5 million.

Senator Sarbanes. And am I correct that most of it was in the private sector? In fact, a very large percentage of it.

Ms. Abraham. That's correct. 3.2 million of that 3.5 million was in the private sector.

Senator Sarbanes. So over 90 percent.

Ms. Abraham. That's right.

Senator Sarbanes. When did the economy last create as many jobs as it did in 1994?

Ms. Abraham. The last time that employment growth on an annual basis was as rapid as it was in 1994, was in 1984.

Senator Sarbanes. So we created more jobs this past year than we had in 10 years.

Ms. Abraham. That is correct.

Senator Sarbanes. How many people are unemployed now in the December survey? How high is the unemployment?

Ms. Abraham. The number of people unemployed was 7.2 million on a seasonally adjusted basis.

Senator Sarbanes. 7.2 million?

Ms. Abraham. That's correct.

Senator Sarbanes. Was it as high as 10 million in the recent past, or nine point something? I'm trying to recall. I don't remember that very well.

Ms. Abraham. At the end of 1993, again, we're mixing old and new survey numbers, it was 8.2 million. At the end of 1992, it was 9.3 million.

Senator Sarbanes. 9.3 at the end of '92. And at the end of '94, it's 7.3.

Is that correct?

Ms. Abraham. If you want to look back to June of '92, it was 9.8 million.

Senator Sarbanes. I thought it was close to 10 at one point. In June of --

Ms. Abraham. '92, it was 9.8 million unemployed people.

Senator Sarbanes. Okay. So in June of '92, it was 9.8 million unemployed people. And today it's 7.3 million?

Ms. Abraham. 7.2 million.

Senator Sarbanes. 7.2. That's in December of 1994.

Ms. Abraham. Correct.

Senator Sarbanes. Okay. So we've gone from 9.8 million unemployed to 7.2 million unemployed.

How about people working part-time for economic reasons? Why don't we take that June month? I take it that's probably --

Ms. Abraham. On that one, I'm afraid we're in a bit tougher situation for making comparisons because effective in January, we changed the way that that was measured.

Prior to January we had not asked explicitly whether people who were working part-time and said they would have preferred full-time work, were actually available for full-time work and in January we modified our definition.

Senator Sarbanes. You shifted the nature of your survey question. Is that right?

Ms. Abraham. We shifted the nature of the survey question.

Senator Sarbanes. Well, why don't you give me -- what was the figure in June of '92?

Ms. Abraham. The total in June of '92 of people who were part-time for economic reasons was 6.2 million, measured the old way.

Senator Sarbanes. Okay. Now when was the last month you measured the old way?

Ms. Abraham. In December of '93, it was 6.2 million. That number held pretty steady for quite a long period of time.

Senator Sarbanes. Okay. Then what was the first month under the new system? January of '94?

Ms. Abraham. That's correct.

Senator Sarbanes. And what was the figure then?

Ms. Abraham. I don't have that figure here -- okay. It was 5.2 million in January and has come down --

Senator Sarbanes. So it went from 6.2 million in December of '93 to 5.2 in January of '94.

Ms. Abraham. As a result of --

Senator Sarbanes. Obviously, as a result of the different survey technique.

Is that correct?

Ms. Abraham. That's correct.

Senator Sarbanes. Well, I mean, assume that.

Ms. Abraham. We believe that that's it.

Senator Sarbanes. All right. What is it now?

Ms. Abraham. 4.4 million.

Senator Sarbanes. So in the course of this year, it's dropped from 5.2 to 4.4.

Ms. Abraham. That's correct.

Senator Sarbanes. Okay. Mr. Chairman, if I could, if the Committee would indulge me just a moment, I want to get the inflation issue here.

As I understand it, during the first 11 months of '94, the Consumer Price Index rose at an annual rate of 2.7 percent, the same inflation rate as in 1993.

Is that correct?

Ms. Abraham. That's correct.

Senator Sarbanes. 1994 is the fourth year in a row with an inflation rate of 3.1 percent or lower.

Ms. Abraham. That's correct.

Senator Sarbanes. In fact, in 1990, it was 6.1 percent. Then it went to 3.1, 2.9, 2.7, and then 2.7 again this year.

Correct?

Ms. Abraham. Correct.

Senator Sarbanes. When did we last have four straight years of inflation of 3.1 percent or less?

Ms. Abraham. It must have been back in the 1960s.

Mr. Dalton. I think it would be the four years ending in 1965.

Senator Sarbanes. Okay. So that's over 30 years ago.

Mr. Dalton. Right. Over the nearly 15-year period from the early '50s to 1965, the CPI only once got as high as 3 percent.

Senator Sarbanes. Right. Well, Mr. Chairman, I'd just make the observation that this is a very strong economic performance right now. We've got the unemployment rate down to 5.4 percent, the lowest in four-and-a-half years almost going towards five years. The inflation is the best performance in 30 years.

Senator Mack. Is that an endorsement of Chairman Greenspan?

Senator Sarbanes. No. I think it's more an endorsement of the policies that were put into place by the Congress. I think we ought to take a little credit on occasion around here ourselves.

Senator Mack. If that's where you want to give it, that would be fine.

Senator Sarbanes. I think it helps to set a benchmark by which to judge what might be coming. And the job growth was the best it's been in 30 years, I think was the figure, wasn't it?

Ms. Abraham. Ten years.

Senator Sarbanes. Ten years. Sorry. 1984.

Senator Mack. 1984, yes.

Senator Sarbanes. Right. Thank you very much. I thank the witnesses.

Senator Mack. Let me ask a series of questions here.

Today's report indicates that the labor force was essentially unchanged, while household employment rose 167,000.

How would you explain the lack of growth in the labor force and what effect would a more typical increase in the labor force have had in the changed monthly unemployment rate?

Ms. Abraham. Well, I guess I think it's important when looking at the data from our monthly household survey, in particular, to try to look at things over a somewhat longer period of time because, although 60,000 households may sound like a lot, that's the number we interview each month, it's still a small enough sample that those numbers, month to month, can move somewhat jerkily.

Over the period from the beginning of the year, the labor force has grown by about 1.1 million.

How does that compare with the growth of the population?

Mr. Plewes. We're gaining on the population now.

Senator Mack. I'm sorry. Say that again.

Mr. Plewes. There's a slowdown in population growth, so we wouldn't expect to have much more than that in labor force growth.

Senator Mack. Are you implying that this may be an indication that we will see similar kinds of situations in the months to come?

Ms. Abraham. I think what he's saying is that over the period from January to the present, labor force growth has been roughly in line with population growth.

Senator Mack. Again, the implication, I think, from what you've said, is don't look to see much growth in the labor force, then, in the months ahead.

Mr. Plewes. To stay even with population growth, one doesn't need so much labor force growth in months ahead. What's happened is that we have done a substitution that labor force has only grown by 1.1 million. We've gained over 2.5 million jobs in the household survey. That has come from subtractions from unemployment. So that hasn't come from the growth in the total.

Senator Mack. Were there any effects from seasonal adjustments or other statistical factors affecting the household data this month?

Ms. Abraham. Not that we are aware of. Again, given that we redesigned the household survey and put the new survey into the field for the first time last January, there is some continuing uncertainty about whether the seasonal factors that we are using are precisely the right seasonal factors.

Senator Mack. Are there any red flags, any concerns that you have at this point?

Ms. Abraham. No, there really are no red flags, no reason to be particularly concerned.

We have, I guess, in looking at the data, become less concerned about that issue over the course of the year.

Senator Mack. All right. What was the unemployment rate for black youths, 16 to 19 years old? And how much progress have they seen over the last 12 months?

Ms. Abraham. The rate for black youth has hovered in the 30s. It was 34.6 percent in December.

Going back to the beginning of the year, it was 32.8 percent. Looking over the course of the whole year, it's gone up and down, but fluctuating within bounds. That's just to say, basically, it's not changed.

Senator Mack. This is really just more for my information, but how are immigrants included in the household survey?

Can illegal immigrants also show up in the household survey?

Ms. Abraham. Well, they could. The way that the survey sample is set up is that it's a housing unit based sample. The Census Bureau interviewers who do the survey for us talk to whomever they find in the housing unit that's in the sample. So if they came to the door and there were a family of illegal immigrants living there, they would be within scope.

Whether they would in fact talk to the interviewer, I guess, is another issue.

Senator Mack. I suppose there would be no way for them to know, would there?

Ms. Abraham. They wouldn't ask. We don't ask. We do ask, I guess, where they were born, but we don't ask about their legal status.

Senator Mack. All right. I may have some further questions in that area in the future. And I really only have a couple more, then I'll turn it over to you.

What was the change in real average weekly earnings reported for November relative to the previous month?

Ms. Abraham. Real average weekly earnings.

Senator Mack. And what was the change relative to the previous November?

Ms. Abraham. Kathy, do you have that handy? This is Kathy MacDonald from our Office of Compensation and Working Conditions.

Senator Mack. Welcome, Kathy.

Ms. Abraham. Constant dollar real weekly earnings were $255.86 in November.

Senator Mack. What was the number again?

Ms. Abraham. $255.86. I don't have the number here for the previous November. For the previous December, it was $257.38. These figures are for production, nonsupervisory workers, and not seasonally adjusted, which may make that comparison a little --

Senator Mack. And again, those are inflation-adjusted?

Ms. Abraham. Those are inflation-adjusted.

Senator Mack. And that would indicate a further decline, then?

Ms. Abraham. That would be consistent with that. These are the numbers from our employer survey, and they cover production nonsupervisory workers.

I would note that the picture that you get from looking at this series may be a little more negative than what you might get from looking at other information. Over the long term, the hourly earnings of production, nonsupervisory workers, that series, has tended to fall relative to other series that we have available.

But, yes, it looks like it's down.

Senator Mack. Thank you.

Representative Saxton. Mr. Chairman, I don't have any other questions at this point, but I do have one observation that I would like to make as I listen to Senator Sarbanes' line of questioning and his great optimism.

I'd like to share that optimism and to say that I'm particularly pleased that the unemployment rate is doing well, as I said before, and I join with Senator Sarbanes in hailing the growth in our economy.

I think it begs a question of this Committee in terms of our responsibility of reporting these findings to our colleagues and to the American people. It begs the question of why all this is happening.

Is it because we are in a cyclical mode? Is it because the economy continues to grow, as it started to in 1991? Is it just an automatic kind of thing or is it because of some trade policies that we put in place? Or is it because of some economic and fiscal policies that we've adopted in the Congress by increasing the tax burden on the American people? Of course, I say this with tongue in cheek. Has that provided some kind of stimulus to the economy to produce this growth?

Or, on the other hand, is it something that is outside of the direct control of the Congress, and that, of course, I refer to the Federal Reserve and the monetary policy that has been pursued since the tax increase of 1993?

Of course, perhaps like you, Mr. Chairman, I am somewhat skeptical of the economy's long-term performance, if we are experiencing this growth because of the latter factor -- that is, the monetary policy pursued since 1993 by the Fed. I think one wants to note for our colleagues and for the American people that there is a lag which we know occurs between growth and monetary stimulus that's provided by the Fed, and we are, in my opinion, at least, currently experiencing some growth that results from some monetary policy of the early 1994, late 1993 timeframe.

If that is true, then we need to be particularly cognizant of the fact that, with current monetary policy having been tightened, which has resulted in higher interest rates, which results in a slowdown in home sales, which has resulted in some concern in the automobile industry and other sectors of the economy, then what is it that we should look for 18 months or two years down the road?

I think that in our discussions relative to fiscal policy, in our discussions relative to other issues that have to do with regulation and other factors that have an effect on the economy, we need to be cognizant that two years ago, certain things happened relative to monetary policy which perhaps are showing up in today's growth numbers, and that the monetary policy that we see today could have some effect some months down the road.

We ought to be in a position to plan our legislative activities with that in mind.

So I appreciate the opportunity to be here this morning. I have no further questions. I congratulate you on the Chairmanship of this panel, and I look forward to working with you over the next two years.

Senator Mack. Thank you very much. Again, I thank you for your information in the report this morning, and I just would remind you again of the first point that I raised.

I just looked back at this article that was in *The Washington Post*. It said that, according to this memorandum about the central oversight group: "In addition to the new central group, each subagency within the department would be required to set up its own oversight team, complete with an oversight coordinator who would work with the department-wide central oversight group and, when necessary, with the rapid response team, if anyone saw the whites of Republicans' eyes."

So I'd be very interested in hearing back from you.

Ms. Abraham. I haven't seen that memo, sir.

Senator Mack. Well, I would be very appreciative of your getting back to me and letting me know how that's going to be handled in your subagency.

Ms. Abraham. I certainly will.

Senator Mack. Thank you very much. The hearing is adjourned.

(Whereupon, at 10:50 a.m., the hearing was adjourned.)

Submissions For The Record

Prepared Statement of Senator Connie Mack, Chairman

I'm happy to welcome everyone to the first meeting of the Joint Economic Committee under full Republican control in 40 years. Needless to say, this will be a novel experience for all of us.

As some of you may know, the Joint Economic Committee was established soon after World War II to provide economic analysis to the Congress as a foundation for fiscal policy. Throughout most of the past nearly five decades, that analysis has supported a major role for the government in the economy.

Under the leadership of Vice-Chairman Saxton and myself, this will change. My conviction is that wealth and prosperity emerge from the spirit of creativity that resides within individuals, not governments. This creativity is enhanced by policies of less taxes, less spending, less government, and more freedom. These will be the watchwords of the JEC during the 104th Congress.

During the first 100 days, my hope is that the JEC will play an important role in helping to pass the Republican economic plan. It is critical that this plan be enacted because it is good for Americans, and the economy will reflect it. Americans want a balanced budget amendment. They want major tax cuts; major spending cuts; regulatory reform; they want the President to have a line-item veto; they want welfare reform. Americans want the Republican economic plan because they know that it will make their economic future much brighter.

As for this morning's hearing, it's a pleasure to welcome Commissioner Katharine Abraham, and we look forward to your unemployment report for December.

I think I can speak for the majority on this panel in saying that we have tremendous respect for the independence and statistical integrity of the Bureau of Labor Statistics and in the high standards established by former Commissioner Janet Norwood. I would encourage you to continue to maintain the independence of the BLS and its data from political forces. If you or anyone else at BLS ever need our help in that regard, please let me know.

I am delighted with much of what is in today's unemployment report. Two hundred fifty-six thousand more Americans at work in December, a drop in the unemployment rate to 5.4 percent, and an increase in manufacturing jobs is decidedly good news. Yet this good news is bittersweet. Despite the fact that more Americans are working, their standards of living are falling.

Even though the economy is still growing, the fact is that this recovery continues to be hollow. Real median incomes of workers and their families -- America's middle class -- have declined over the past two years.

This gap between job growth and actual incomes is due in large part to high-tax, big-government policies the economy is saddled with. As always, the unintended consequences of taxation and regulation are lower incomes and fewer opportunities for the middle class.

The unemployment data released this morning do not change this picture. The middle class feels itself trapped in what I call a "treadmill economy."

The latest available Census data for 1993 show that real median earnings for both male and female workers actually declined in 1993.

BLS data show that real median weekly earnings declined between the third quarters of 1993 and 1994. These are not the resultss one would expect from an economy in which job quality was rising. This, in turn, raises questions about the quality of the jobs that are being produced. And even the Clinton Administration now concedes that the middle class has not benefitted from the economic growth that is reflected in the GDP numbers.

I imagine that my Democratic colleagues will say that the slowdown in job growth is the direct result of Federal Reserve policy -- that the Fed is choking the economy. But I would argue that the real culprit behind these figures is big government and the legacy of Democratic policies.

High taxes and hyper-regulation always bring an economy to its knees. And using the Fed to paper over these problems is a recipe for diaster. That is why revamping the Humphrey-Hawkins Act is high on my list of priorities.

This brings me to the Republican economic plan and why today's unemployment report is more evidence of why that plan must be enacted quickly.

Lower taxes, spending cuts, regulatory reform, elimination of unfunded mandates, and welfare reform are a recipe for prosperity. Our agenda will get the American people off the treadmill and the economy into the fast lane.

PREPARED STATEMENT OF REPRESENTATIVE JIM SAXTON, VICE CHAIRMAN

Thank you, Mr. Chairman. And Commissioner Abraham, thank you for your welcome report this morning. We are all pleased that the unemployment rate has declined to 5.4 percent, and the strong increase in employment last month certainly represents glad tidings.

This strong employment report is welcome in another important way as well. It means that we in Congress have some breathing room to take a longer perspective on this economy than we usually do as we set about the important task of crafting economic policy to improve the long-run economic outlook. For make no mistake about it, few economists -- and more importantly few workers -- feel confident about the intermediate and long-run economic outlook.

I continue to believe that today's strong economy is the direct result of past monetary policy that was too loose and that today's apparent economic strength is not sustainable over the longer run. Most economists show growth slacking next year and some even warn of a recession in 1996 if the Fed continues to tighten monetary policy.

The good news is, however, that the Contract With America is designed to improve long-run economic performance, not to give the economy a short-run jolt. Today's strong report means that we don't have to operate in a crisis atmosphere as we seem to much too often around here. We have the ability to put in place tax and regulatory policies that are aimed to raise the long-run, noninflationary growth capacity of the economy, and, Mr. Chairman, I for one am anxious to get about that business.

PREPARED STATEMENT OF KATHARINE G. ABRAHAM

Together with Press Release No. 95-02 entitled, "The Employment Situation: December 1994," Bureau of I abor Statistics, Department of Labor, January 6, 1995

Advance copies of this statement are made available to the press under lock-up conditions with the explicit understanding that the data are embargoed until 8:30 a.m. Eastern time.

. Statement of

Katharine G. Abraham
Commissioner
Bureau of Labor Statistics

before the

Joint Economic Committee

UNITED STATES CONGRESS

January 6, 1995

Mr. Chairman and Members of the Committee:

I appreciate this opportunity to comment on the labor market data released earlier this morning.

December data sustained the pattern of labor market improvements that was fairly pervasive throughout 1994. Payroll employment continued to advance, increasing by 256,000 over the month. Unemployment remained on its downward trend; at 5.4 percent, the unemployment rate was 1.3 percentage points below its level at the beginning of 1994.

December's gain in employment, as measured by our survey of businesses, brings the increase in payroll jobs for all of 1994 to 3-1/2 million. This exceeded the prior year's gain by over a million and was the largest in the past decade.

Factory employment rose by 54,000 in December, with gains widespread throughout the individual manufacturing industries. The largest increases occurred in fabricated metals and electronic equipment. Manufacturing job growth totaled nearly 300,000 for the year as a whole, compared with a loss of 130,000 in 1993. The extraordinarily high levels of weekly hours and overtime during 1994 provide additional evidence of the strength in the demand for labor in manufacturing. Although construction employment showed little movement in December, for all of 1994, employment in the industry rose by about 300,000, the largest annual gain in 10 years.

The services industry added 110,000 jobs in December, with increases in business, health, and social services. Over the year, employment growth in services totaled 1.6 million. Retail trade also had substantial employment gains both in December (91,000) and over the year (nearly 800,000). Most of December's gain was in eating and drinking places, which appear to have had a strong holiday season. Holiday-related increases in package delivery and traveling lie behind the December employment increase in the transportation industry, and holiday-related shipping also contributed to an over-the-month gain in Federal government (postal) employment. Over the year, however, the number of

Federal jobs has declined by about 50,000 (and would have declined even more had the Postal Service been excluded). Local governments (excluding education) shed 57,000 jobs in December, as workers brought on for the November elections were no longer on the payrolls. Absent the inclusion of these temporary positions in the November job count, the December employment increase would have been larger and that for November correspondingly smaller.

As is our normal practice at the end of the year, the seasonally adjusted estimates from the household survey have been revised to reflect updated seasonal factors. Because of the major redesign of the household survey that was implemented in January 1994, this year we have revised only data for the last 12 months.

Like the estimates from the employer survey, the household survey data show substantial improvement in the labor market during 1994. As I mentioned earlier, the unemployment rate dropped 1.3 percentage points from 6.7 percent in January to 5.4 percent in December, as the number of unemployed persons declined by 1.6 million. Jobless rates improved during the year for adults and teenagers as well as for whites, blacks, and Hispanics. In addition, the number of persons working part time when they would have preferred full-time work declined by nearly 650,000. Since January, total employment has risen by 2.7 million, raising the proportion of the population with jobs to a very high

63.0 percent. The labor force rose by 1.1 million over the January-December period.

In summary, the labor market showed strength in December as it did throughout 1994. Employment, as measured by both of our monthly surveys, has increased substantially over the year and unemployment has fallen.

My colleagues and I now would be glad to answer any questions you might have.

News
United States Department of Labor
Bureau of Labor Statistics Washington, D.C. 20212

Technical information:
Household data:
National (202) 606-6378
606-6373
State 606-6392
Establishment data: 606-6555
Media contact: 606-5902

USDL 95-02

Transmission of material in this release is embargoed until 8:30 A.M. (EST), Friday, January 6, 1995.

THE EMPLOYMENT SITUATION: DECEMBER 1994

The nation's job market improved further in December, the Bureau of Labor Statistics of the U.S. Department of Labor reported today. The unemployment rate continued its downward trend, reaching 5.4 percent in December; it has declined by 1.3 percentage points since January 1994.

The employer survey showed an increase of 256,000 nonfarm payroll jobs in December; this followed a gain of 488,000 (as revised) in November. Total employment—as measured by the

Chart 1. Unemployment rate, seasonally adjusted, January 1992 - December 1994
Percent

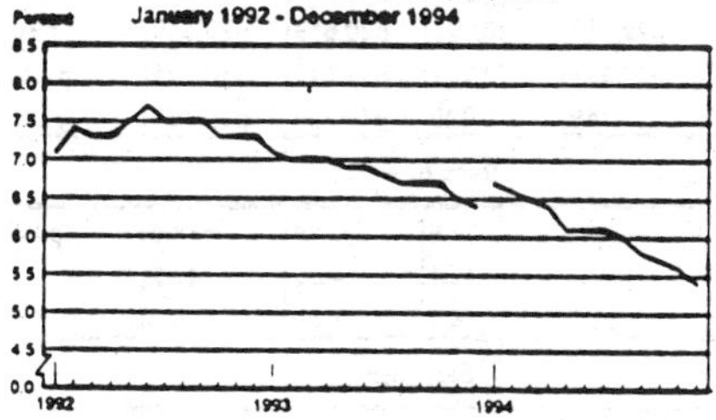

Chart 2. Nonfarm payroll employment, seasonally adjusted, January 1992 - December 1994
Millions

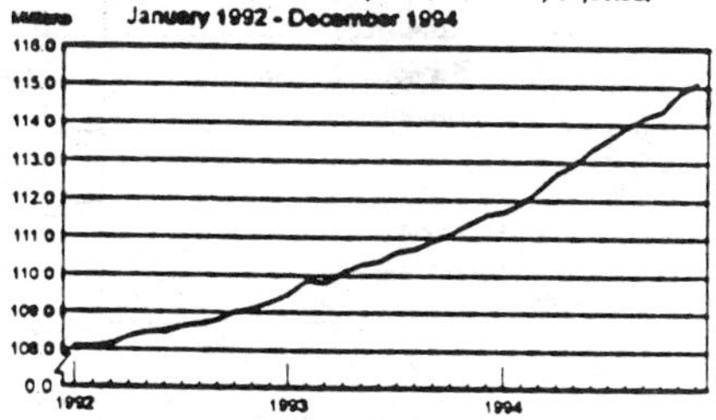

This release incorporates annual revisions in seasonally adjusted unemployment and other labor force series derived from the household survey. Information on the revisions appears on page 5.

Data from the household survey for 1994 are not directly comparable with data for 1993 and earlier years because of the implementation in January 1994 of a major redesign of the survey and the introduction of 1990 census-based population controls, adjusted for the estimated undercount in the decennial census. In addition, the 1994 data may have been affected by the transition to the redesigned survey. For example, seasonal factors, of necessity, were computed based largely on data collected in the survey prior to its revision, and these factors may not fully capture the pattern of seasonality in current data. Hence, over-the-month comparisons of labor force estimates should be made with caution. For additional information on the redesign, see "Revisions in the Current Population Survey Effective January 1994" in the February 1994 issue of *Employment and Earnings*.

Table A. Major indicators of labor market activity, seasonally adjusted

(Numbers in thousands)

Category	Quarterly averages 1994		Monthly data 1994			Nov.-Dec. change
	III	IV	Oct.	Nov.	Dec.	
HOUSEHOLD DATA	Labor force status					
Civilian labor force	131,050	131,696	131,646	131,718	131,725	7
Employment	123,207	124,371	124,141	124,403	124,570	167
Unemployment	7,843	7,325	7,505	7,315	7,155	-160
Not in labor force	66,000	65,904	65,784	65,889	66,040	151
	Unemployment rates					
All workers	6.0	5.6	5.7	5.6	5.4	-0.2
Adult men	5.3	4.9	5.0	4.9	4.7	-.2
Adult women	5.3	4.9	5.0	5.0	4.7	-.3
Teenagers	17.5	16.7	17.1	15.8	17.2	1.4
White	5.2	4.9	5.0	4.8	4.8	.0
Black	11.1	10.4	11.1	10.5	9.8	-.7
Hispanic origin	10.0	9.1	9.4	8.8	9.2	.4
ESTABLISHMENT DATA	Employment					
Nonfarm employment	113,908	p114,759	114,348	p114,836	p115,092	p256
Goods-producing [1]	23,634	p23,804	23,715	p23,825	p23,871	p46
Construction	4,953	p5,021	4,974	p5,047	p5,041	p-6
Manufacturing	18,079	p18,186	18,142	p18,181	p18,235	p54
Service-producing [1]	90,274	p90,955	90,633	p91,011	p91,221	p210
Retail trade	20,420	p20,617	20,523	p20,619	p20,710	p91
Services	32,031	p32,388	32,231	p32,411	p32,521	p110
Government	19,087	p19,159	19,120	p19,194	p19,164	p-30
	Hours of work [2]					
Total private	34.5	p34.7	34.9	p34.6	p34.6	p0.0
Manufacturing	42.0	p42.2	42.1	p42.2	p42.2	p.0
Overtime	4.6	p4.7	4.7	p4.7	p4.8	p.1
	Earnings [2]					
Average hourly earnings, total private	$11.14	p$11.25	$11.25	p$11.23	p$11.26	p$0.03
Average weekly earnings, total private	384.59	p390.26	392.63	p388.56	p389.60	p1.04

[1] Includes other industries, not shown separately.

[2] Data relate to private production or nonsupervisory workers.

p = preliminary.

NOTE: Household data for 1994 are not directly comparable with data for 1993 and earlier years. For additional information, see "Revisions in the Current Population Survey Effective January 1994" in the February 1994 issue of *Employment and Earnings*. Seasonally adjusted data for 1994 have been revised.

household survey—continued to trend upward. Both surveys recorded large employment gains in 1994. For example, over-the-year growth in the payroll job count was the largest in a decade.

Unemployment (Household Survey Data)

Both the number of persons unemployed (7.2 million in December) and the unemployment rate (5.4 percent) continued to trend downward. About 1.6 million fewer persons were unemployed in December than in January 1994.

Unemployment rates for both adult women and men each fell slightly in December to 4.7 percent, while the rate for teenagers edged up to 17.2 percent. The jobless rate for blacks (9.8 percent) inched down from the prior month; the rate for whites (4.8 percent) was the same as in November, while that for Hispanics (9.2 percent) was little changed over the month. Jobless rates for all of these major labor force groups have declined since January 1994. (See tables A-1 and A-2.)

Total Employment and the Labor Force (Household Survey Data)

At 124.6 million (seasonally adjusted) in December, the number of employed persons continued its upward trend. Total employment has increased by 2.7 million since the beginning of 1994. The employment-population ratio—the proportion of the working-age population with jobs—remained at 63.0 percent in December, 0.8 percentage point higher than in January. (See tables A-1 and A-2.)

The number of persons employed part time for economic reasons (4.4 million) and the number of voluntary part-time workers (17.6 million) were little changed in December. (See table A-3.) A total of 7.5 million persons (not seasonally adjusted), or 6.0 percent of the total employed, held two or more jobs (table A-8).

The number of persons in the civilian labor force, at 131.7 million, was about unchanged for the second straight month. This followed an increase of 1.1 million between June and October. The labor force had shown little movement during the first half of the year. (See table A-1.)

Persons Not in the Labor Force (Household Survey Data)

The number of persons with a marginal attachment to the labor force—those who wanted and were available for work, but were no longer actively looking after having searched sometime in the past 12 months—was 1.8 million (not seasonally adjusted) in December. Of that total, the number who were not looking because they felt that there were no jobs available for them—discouraged workers—was 445,000. (See table A-8.)

Industry Payroll Employment (Establishment Survey Data)

Nonfarm payroll employment rose by 256,000 in December, following a gain of 488,000 in November (as revised). The overall employment growth in November had been inflated by the hiring of large numbers of temporary election workers. Their absence from payrolls in December similarly depressed the job growth registered in that month. Large over-the-month increases occurred in the private sector, particularly in services, retail trade, and manufacturing. Nonfarm employment increased by 3.5 million during all of 1994. (See table B-1.)

The services industry added 110,000 jobs in December. Half the gain was in business services, mostly in the personnel supply and computer services components. Smaller, but noteworthy, increases also occurred in health and social services. These two industries and business services have added large numbers of jobs throughout much of the year, as employment in the services industry as a whole rose by 1.6 million.

Retail trade employment rose by 91,000 over the month, following a similar increase in November (96,000, as revised). Most of the December gain was in eating and drinking establishments, while smaller increases occurred in food stores, automotive dealers and service stations, and furniture stores.

Manufacturing employment rose by 54,000 in December. This is the third large monthly increase in a row and represents an acceleration in the upward trend that began in September 1993. Since then, factory employment has risen by 301,000. Over the month, factory job growth was widespread, with the largest gains occurring in fabricated metals, electronic equipment, printing and publishing (including the return of striking workers), and rubber and miscellaneous plastics products.

The strong growth trend in wholesale trade continued in December with an increase of 11,000. Employment in transportation and public utilities also rose in December (by 25,000), reflecting larger-than-usual hiring in the transportation industry to help with holiday travel and package delivery. Although construction employment failed to grow in December, 300,000 jobs were added in 1994, for the strongest showing in a decade.

Employment decreased in government in December. A decline of 57,000 workers in local government except education, reflecting the dismissal of temporary election workers, more than offset increased hiring by the Postal Service.

Weekly Hours (Establishment Survey Data)

The average workweek for production or nonsupervisory workers on private nonfarm payrolls held at 34.6 hours in December, seasonally adjusted. The manufacturing workweek, at 42.2 hours, also was unchanged over the month, while factory overtime hours edged up to 4.8 hours. Since last spring, both the factory workweek and overtime hours have been at or near post-World War II record highs. (See table B-2.)

Reflecting the increase in payroll employment, the index of aggregate weekly hours of production or nonsupervisory workers on private nonfarm payrolls was up by 0.3 percent in December to 131.1 (1982=100), seasonally adjusted. The index for manufacturing rose 0.7 percent to 107.6. (See table B-5.)

Hourly and Weekly Earnings (Establishment Survey Data)

Average hourly earnings for production or nonsupervisory workers on private nonfarm payrolls rose 3 cents in December to $11.26, seasonally adjusted. Average weekly earnings increased 0.3 percent to $389.60. Over the year, average hourly earnings rose by 2.8 percent, while average weekly earnings increased 3.0 percent. (See table B-3.)

The Employment Situation for January 1995 will be released on Friday, February 3, at 8:30 A.M. (EST).

Revision of Seasonally Adjusted Household Survey Data

At the end of each calendar year, BLS routinely updates the seasonal adjustment factors for the labor force series derived from the Current Population Survey (the CPS, also referred to as the "household survey") to incorporate the experience of that year. Because of the changes introduced into the CPS at the beginning of 1994, only seasonally adjusted data for that year have been revised. Normally, data for the most recent 5 years are subject to revision. (Seasonally adjusted establishment data will be revised in June, concurrently with the introduction of annual benchmark adjustments.)

Table B summarizes the effects of the revisions on the monthly overall unemployment rates in 1994. Rates for 6 months were revised, each by 0.1 percentage point. Revised seasonally adjusted data for major labor force series for January through December 1994 are presented in table C.

The January 1995 issue of Employment and Earnings will contain the seasonal adjustment factors that will be used to calculate the civilian labor force and other major series for the January-June period of 1995. The publication also will contain a description of the current seasonal adjustment methodology and revised data for the 12 months and 4 quarters of 1994 for all regularly published tables containing seasonally adjusted household survey data. Microcomputer diskettes of historical seasonally adjusted data (monthly and quarterly) may be purchased from BLS; contact Gloria P. Green on 202-606-6373.

Table B. Seasonally adjusted unemployment rates in 1994 and change due to revision

Month	As first computed	As revised	Change
January	6.7	6.7	.0
February	6.5	6.6	0.1
March	6.5	6.5	.0
April	6.4	6.4	.0
May	6.0	6.1	.1
June	6.0	6.1	.1
July	6.1	6.1	.0
August	6.1	6.0	-.1
September	5.9	5.8	-.1
October	5.8	5.7	-.1
November	5.6	5.6	.0
December	*5.4	5.4	.0

*Not published

Table C. Employment status of the civilian population by sex and age

(Numbers in thousands)

Employment status, sex, and age	1994											
	Jan.	Feb.	Mar.	Apr.	May	June	July	Aug.	Sept.	Oct.	Nov	Dec.
TOTAL												
Civilian noninstitutional population[1]	195,953	196,090	196,213	196,363	196,510	196,693	196,859	197,043	197,248	197,430	197,607	197,765
Civilian labor force	130,843	130,784	130,708	130,787	130,699	130,538	130,774	131,086	131,291	131,646	131,718	131,725
Participation rate	66.7	66.7	66.6	66.6	66.5	66.4	66.4	66.5	66.6	66.7	66.7	66.6
Employed	121,903	122,208	122,160	122,402	122,703	122,635	122,781	123,197	123,644	124,141	124,403	124,570
Employment-population ratio	62.2	62.3	62.3	62.3	62.4	62.3	62.4	62.5	62.7	62.9	63.0	63.0
Unemployed	8,740	8,576	8,546	8,385	7,996	7,903	7,993	7,889	7,647	7,505	7,315	7,155
Unemployment rate	6.7	6.6	6.5	6.4	6.1	6.1	6.1	6.0	5.8	5.7	5.6	5.4
Men, 20 years and over												
Civilian noninstitutional population[1]	86,778	86,820	86,900	86,946	87,000	87,095	87,123	87,248	87,321	87,439	87,529	87,617
Civilian labor force	66,800	66,753	66,748	66,741	66,652	66,602	66,747	66,817	66,909	67,177	67,345	67,450
Participation rate	77.0	76.9	76.8	76.8	76.6	76.5	76.6	76.6	76.6	76.8	76.9	77.0
Employed	62,745	62,787	62,877	62,959	63,080	63,043	63,076	63,271	63,517	63,820	64,051	64,281
Employment-population ratio	72.3	72.3	72.4	72.4	72.5	72.4	72.4	72.5	72.7	73.0	73.2	73.4
Agriculture	2,338	2,339	2,357	2,362	2,384	2,334	2,314	2,377	2,293	2,329	2,377	2,410
Nonagricultural industries	60,407	60,428	60,520	60,597	60,696	60,709	60,762	60,894	61,224	61,491	61,674	61,871
Unemployed	4,056	3,966	3,871	3,782	3,572	3,559	3,671	3,546	3,392	3,357	3,294	3,169
Unemployment rate	6.1	6.0	5.8	5.7	5.4	5.3	5.5	5.3	5.1	5.0	4.9	4.7
Women, 20 years and over												
Civilian noninstitutional population[1]	95,100	95,159	95,225	95,282	95,329	95,407	95,489	95,544	95,658	95,729	95,821	95,873
Civilian labor force	56,373	56,592	56,511	56,466	56,545	56,384	56,536	56,747	57,031	56,951	56,984	56,725
Participation rate	59.3	59.5	59.3	59.3	59.3	59.1	59.2	59.4	59.6	59.5	59.5	59.2
Employed	53,067	53,355	53,176	53,318	53,481	53,328	53,541	53,722	54,044	54,090	54,129	54,037
Employment-population ratio	55.8	56.1	55.8	56.0	56.1	55.9	56.1	56.2	56.5	56.5	56.5	56 [illegible]
Agriculture	751	769	775	833	789	739	790	815	847	863	850	8[illegible]
Nonagricultural industries	52,316	52,586	52,401	52,485	52,692	52,589	52,751	52,907	53,197	53,227	53,279	53,155
Unemployed	3,306	3,237	3,335	3,148	3,064	3,056	2,995	3,025	2,987	2,861	2,855	2,688
Unemployment rate	5.9	5.7	5.9	5.6	5.4	5.4	5.3	5.3	5.2	5.0	5.0	4.7
Both sexes, 16 to 19 years												
Civilian noninstitutional population[1]	14,086	14,111	14,087	14,135	14,181	14,191	14,267	14,251	14,269	14,261	14,257	14,274
Civilian labor force	7,470	7,439	7,447	7,580	7,502	7,552	7,491	7,522	7,351	7,518	7,389	7,550
Participation rate	53.1	52.7	52.9	53.6	52.9	53.2	52.5	52.8	51.5	52.7	51.8	52.9
Employed	6,091	6,086	6,107	6,125	6,142	6,264	6,164	6,204	6,083	6,231	6,223	6,252
Employment-population ratio	43.3	43.1	43.4	43.3	43.3	44.1	43.2	43.5	42.6	43.7	43.6	43.8
Agriculture	239	260	264	243	240	221	229	244	271	302	273	240
Nonagricultural industries	5,852	5,826	5,843	5,882	5,902	6,043	5,935	5,960	5,812	5,929	5,950	6,012
Unemployed	1,379	1,353	1,340	1,455	1,360	1,288	1,327	1,318	1,268	1,287	1,166	1,298
Unemployment rate	18.5	18.2	18.0	19.2	18.1	17.1	17.7	17.5	17.2	17.1	15.8	17.2

[1] The population figures are not adjusted for seasonal variation.

NOTE: Data for 1994 are not directly comparable with data for 1993 and earlier years. For additional information, see "Revisions in the Current Population Survey Effective January 1994" in the February 1994 issue of *Employment and Earnings*.

Explanatory Note

This news release presents statistics from two major surveys, the Current Population Survey (household survey) and the Current Employment Statistics survey (establishment survey). The household survey provides the information on the labor force, employment, and unemployment that appears in the A tables, marked HOUSEHOLD DATA. It is a sample survey of about 60,000 households conducted by the Bureau of the Census for the Bureau of Labor Statistics (BLS).

The establishment survey provides the information on the employment, hours, and earnings of workers on nonfarm payrolls that appears in the B tables, marked ESTABLISHMENT DATA. This information is collected from payroll records by BLS in cooperation with State agencies. In March 1993, the sample included over 390,000 establishments employing over 47 million people.

For both surveys, the data for a given month relate to a particular week or pay period. In the household survey, the reference week is generally the calendar week that contains the 12th day of the month. In the establishment survey, the reference period is the pay period including the 12th, which may or may not correspond directly to the calendar week.

Coverage, definitions, and differences between surveys

Household survey. The sample is selected to reflect the entire civilian noninstitutional population. Based on responses to a series of questions on work and job search activities, each person 16 years and over in a sample household is classified as employed, unemployed, or not in the labor force.

People are classified as *employed* if they did any work at all as paid employees during the reference week; worked in their own business, profession, or on their own farm; or worked without pay at least 15 hours in a family business or farm. People are also counted as employed if they were temporarily absent from their jobs because of illness, bad weather, vacation, labor-management disputes, or personal reasons.

People are classified as *unemployed* if they meet all of the following criteria: They had no employment during the reference week; they were available for work at that time; and they made specific efforts to find employment sometime during the 4-week period ending with the reference week. Persons laid off from a job and expecting recall need not be looking for work to be counted as unemployed. The unemployment data derived from the household survey in no way depend upon the eligibility for or receipt of unemployment insurance benefits.

The *civilian labor force* is the sum of employed and unemployed persons. Those not classified as employed or unemployed are *not in the labor force*. The *unemployment rate* is the number unemployed as a percent of the labor force. The *labor force participation rate* is the labor force as a percent of the population, and the *employment-population ratio* is the employed as a percent of the population.

Establishment survey. The sample establishments are drawn from private nonfarm businesses such as factories, offices, and stores, as well as Federal, State, and local government entities. *Employees on nonfarm payrolls* are those who received pay for any part of the reference pay period, including persons on paid leave. Persons are counted in each job they hold. *Hours and earnings* data are for private businesses and relate only to production workers in the goods-producing sector and nonsupervisory workers in the service-producing sector.

Differences in employment estimates. The numerous conceptual and methodological differences between the household and establishment surveys result in important distinctions in the employment estimates derived from the surveys. Among these are:

- The household survey includes agricultural workers, the self-employed, unpaid family workers, and private household workers among the employed. These groups are excluded from the establishment survey.
- The household survey includes people on unpaid leave among the employed. The establishment survey does not.
- The household survey is limited to workers 16 years of age and older. The establishment survey is not limited by age.
- The household survey has no duplication of individuals, because individuals are counted only once, even if they hold more than one job. In the establishment survey, employees working at more than one job and thus appearing on more than one payroll would be counted separately for each appearance.

Other differences between the two surveys are described in "Comparing Employment Estimates from Household and Payroll Surveys," which may be obtained from BLS upon request.

Seasonal adjustment

Over the course of a year, the size of the nation's labor force and the levels of employment and unemployment undergo sharp fluctuations due to such seasonal events as changes in weather, reduced or expanded production, harvests, major holidays, and the opening and closing of schools. The effect of such seasonal variation can be very large; seasonal fluctuations may account for as much as 95 percent of the month-to-month changes in unemployment.

Because these seasonal events follow a more or less regular pattern each year, their influence on statistical trends can be eliminated by adjusting the statistics from month to month. These adjustments make nonseasonal developments, such as declines in economic activity or increases in the participation of women in the labor force, easier to spot. For example, the large number of youth entering the labor force each June is likely to obscure any other changes that have taken place relative to May, making it difficult to determine if the level of economic activity has risen or declined. However, because the effect of students finishing school in previous years is known, the statistics for the current year can be adjusted to allow for a comparable change. Insofar as the seasonal adjustment is made correctly, the adjusted figure provides a more useful tool with which to analyze changes in economic activity.

In both the household and establishment surveys, most seasonally adjusted series are independently adjusted. However, the adjusted series for many major estimates, such as total payroll employment, employment in most major industry divisions, total employment, and unemployment are computed by aggregating independently adjusted component series. For example, total unemployment is derived by summing the adjusted series for four major age-sex components; this differs from the unemployment estimate that would be obtained by directly adjusting the total or by combining the duration, reasons, or more detailed age categories.

The numerical factors used to make the seasonal adjustments are recalculated twice a year. For the household survey, the factors are calculated for the January-June period and again for the July-December period. For the establishment survey, updated factors for seasonal adjustment are calculated for the May-October period and introduced along with new benchmarks, and again for the November-April period. In both surveys, revisions to historical data are made once a year.

Reliability of the estimates

Statistics based on the household and establishment surveys are subject to both sampling and nonsampling error. When a sample rather than the entire population is surveyed, there is a chance that the sample estimates may differ from the "true" population values they represent. The exact difference, or *sampling error*, varies depending on the particular sample selected, and this variability is measured by the standard error of the estimate. There is about a 90-percent chance, or level of confidence, that an estimate based on a sample will differ by no more than 1.6 standard errors from the "true" population value because of sampling error. BLS analyses are generally conducted at the 90-percent level of confidence.

For example, the confidence interval for the monthly change in total employment from the household survey is on the order of plus or minus 359,000. Suppose the estimate of total employment increases by 100,000 from one month to the next. The 90-percent confidence interval on the monthly change would range from -259,000 to 459,000 (100,000 +/- 359,000). These figures do not mean that the sample results are off by these magnitudes, but rather that there is about a 90-percent chance that the "true" over-the-month change lies within this interval. Since this range includes values of less than zero, we could not say with confidence that employment had, in fact, increased. If, however, the reported employment rise was half a million, then all of the values within the 90-percent confidence interval would be greater than zero. In this case, it is likely (at least a 90-percent chance) that an employment rise had, in fact, occurred. The 90-percent confidence interval for the monthly change in unemployment is +/- 256,000, and for the monthly change in the unemployment rate it is +/- .22 percentage point.

In general, estimates involving many individuals or establishments have lower standard errors (relative to the size of the estimate) than estimates which are based on a small number of observations. The precision of estimates is also improved when the data are cumulated over time such as for quarterly and annual averages. The seasonal adjustment process can also improve the stability of the monthly estimates.

The household and establishment surveys are also affected by *nonsampling error*. Nonsampling errors can occur for many reasons, including the failure to sample a segment of the population, inability to obtain information for all respondents in the sample, inability or unwillingness of respondents to provide correct information on a timely basis, mistakes made by respondents, and errors made in the collection or processing of the data.

For example, in the establishment survey, estimates for the most recent 2 months are based on substantially incomplete returns; for this reason, these estimates are labeled preliminary in the tables. It is only after two successive revisions to a monthly estimate, when nearly all sample reports have been received, that the estimate is considered final.

Another major source of nonsampling error in the establishment survey is the inability to capture, on a timely basis, employment generated by new firms. To correct for this systematic underestimation of employment growth (and other sources of error), a process known as bias adjustment is included in the survey's estimating procedures, whereby a specified number of jobs is added to the monthly sample-based change. The size of the monthly bias adjustment is based largely on past relationships between the sample-based estimates of employment and the total counts of employment described below.

The sample-based estimates from the establishment survey are adjusted once a year (on a lagged basis) to universe counts of payroll employment obtained from administrative records of the unemployment insurance program. The difference between the March sample-based employment estimates and the March universe counts is known as a benchmark revision, and serves as a rough proxy for total survey error. The new benchmarks also incorporate changes in the classification of industries. Over the past decade, the benchmark revision for total nonfarm employment has averaged 0.2 percent, ranging from zero to 0.6 percent.

Additional statistics and other information

More comprehensive statistics are contained in *Employment and Earnings*, published each month by BLS. It is available for $14.00 per issue or $29.00 per year from the U.S. Government Printing Office, Washington, DC 20402. All orders must be prepaid by sending a check or money order payable to the Superintendent of Documents, or by charging to Mastercard or Visa.

Employment and Earnings also provides measures of sampling error for the household survey data published in this release. For unemployment and other labor force categories, these measures appear in tables 1-B through 1-H of its "Explanatory Notes." Measures of the reliability of the data drawn from the establishment survey and the actual amounts of revision due to benchmark adjustments are provided in tables 2-B through 2-G of that publication.

Information in this release will be made available to sensory impaired individuals upon request. Voice phone: 202-606-STAT; TDD phone: 202-606-5897; TDD message referral phone: 1-800-326-2577.

HOUSEHOLD DATA

Table A-1. Employment status of the civilian population by sex and age

(Numbers in thousands)

Employment status, sex, and age	Not seasonally adjusted			Seasonally adjusted[2]					
	Dec. 1993	Nov. 1994[1]	Dec. 1994	Dec. 1993	Aug. 1994[1]	Sept. 1994	Oct. 1994	Nov. 1994	Dec. 1994
TOTAL									
Civilian noninstitutional population	194,472	197,807	197,765	194,472	197,043	197,248	197,430	197,607	197,765
Civilian labor force	128,401	131,869	131,418	128,898	131,086	131,291	131,646	131,718	131,725
Participation rate	66.0	66.7	66.5	66.3	66.5	66.6	66.7	66.7	66.6
Employed	120,636	124,896	124,729	120,661	123,197	123,644	124,141	124,403	124,570
Employment-population ratio	62.0	63.2	63.1	62.0	62.5	62.7	62.9	63.0	63.0
Agriculture	2,837	3,480	3,285	3,096	3,436	3,411	3,494	3,500	3,532
Nonagricultural industries	117,800	121,416	121,444	117,565	119,761	120,233	120,647	120,903	121,038
Unemployed	7,764	6,973	6,690	8,237	7,889	7,647	7,505	7,315	7,155
Unemployment rate	6.0	5.3	5.1	6.4	6.0	5.8	5.7	5.6	5.4
Not in labor force	66,071	65,738	66,347	65,574	65,957	65,957	65,784	65,889	66,040
Men, 16 years and over									
Civilian noninstitutional population	93,116	94,768	94,851	93,116	94,469	94,576	94,671	94,768	94,851
Civilian labor force	69,319	71,013	71,060	69,813	70,741	70,791	71,133	71,168	71,379
Participation rate	74.4	74.9	74.9	75.0	74.9	74.9	75.1	75.1	75.3
Employed	64,919	67,313	67,292	65,259	66,458	66,682	67,059	67,244	67,483
Employment-population ratio	69.7	71.0	70.9	70.1	70.3	70.5	70.8	71.0	71.1
Unemployed	4,399	3,700	3,767	4,554	4,283	4,109	4,074	3,924	3,896
Unemployment rate	6.3	5.2	5.3	6.5	6.1	5.8	5.7	5.5	5.5
Men, 20 years and over									
Civilian noninstitutional population	86,373	87,529	87,617	86,373	87,248	87,321	87,439	87,529	87,617
Civilian labor force	66,072	67,364	67,388	66,321	66,817	66,909	67,177	67,345	67,450
Participation rate	76.5	77.0	76.9	76.8	76.6	76.6	76.8	76.9	77.0
Employed	62,266	64,239	64,263	62,444	63,271	63,517	63,820	64,051	64,281
Employment-population ratio	72.1	73.4	73.3	72.3	72.5	72.7	73.0	73.2	73.4
Agriculture	2,146	2,402	2,291	2,300	2,377	2,293	2,329	2,377	2,410
Nonagricultural industries	60,119	61,837	61,972	60,144	60,894	61,224	61,491	61,674	61,871
Unemployed	3,807	3,125	3,125	3,877	3,546	3,392	3,357	3,294	3,169
Unemployment rate	5.8	4.6	4.6	5.8	5.3	5.1	5.0	4.9	4.7
Women, 16 years and over									
Civilian noninstitutional population	101,356	102,839	102,913	101,356	102,575	102,672	102,758	102,839	102,913
Civilian labor force	59,082	60,856	60,359	59,085	60,345	60,500	60,513	60,550	60,346
Participation rate	58.3	59.2	58.7	58.3	58.8	58.9	58.9	58.9	58.6
Employed	55,717	57,584	57,437	55,402	56,739	56,962	57,082	57,159	57,087
Employment-population ratio	55.0	56.0	55.8	54.7	55.3	55.5	55.5	55.6	55.5
Unemployed	3,365	3,272	2,922	3,683	3,606	3,538	3,431	3,391	3,259
Unemployment rate	5.7	5.4	4.8	6.2	6.0	5.8	5.7	5.6	5.4
Women, 20 years and over									
Civilian noninstitutional population	94,784	95,821	95,873	94,784	95,544	95,658	95,729	95,821	95,873
Civilian labor force	55,931	57,444	56,871	55,783	56,747	57,031	56,951	56,984	56,725
Participation rate	59.0	59.9	59.3	58.9	59.4	59.6	59.5	59.5	59.2
Employed	52,978	54,667	54,404	52,631	53,722	54,044	54,090	54,129	54,037
Employment-population ratio	55.9	57.1	56.7	55.5	56.2	56.5	56.5	56.5	56.4
Agriculture	548	844	824	599	815	847	863	850	882
Nonagricultural industries	52,431	53,823	53,580	52,032	52,907	53,197	53,227	53,279	53,155
Unemployed	2,952	2,778	2,467	3,152	3,025	2,987	2,861	2,855	2,688
Unemployment rate	5.3	4.8	4.3	5.7	5.3	5.2	5.0	5.0	4.7
Both sexes, 16 to 19 years									
Civilian noninstitutional population	13,336	14,257	14,274	13,335	14,251	14,269	14,261	14,257	14,274
Civilian labor force	6,398	7,061	7,159	6,794	7,522	7,351	7,518	7,389	7,550
Participation rate	48.0	49.5	50.2	50.9	52.8	51.5	52.7	51.8	52.9
Employed	5,393	5,990	6,062	5,586	6,204	6,083	6,231	6,223	6,252
Employment-population ratio	40.4	42.0	42.5	41.9	43.5	42.6	43.7	43.6	43.8
Agriculture	144	234	171	197	244	271	302	273	240
Nonagricultural industries	5,250	5,756	5,891	5,389	5,960	5,812	5,929	5,950	6,012
Unemployed	1,005	1,071	1,097	1,208	1,318	1,268	1,287	1,166	1,298
Unemployment rate	15.7	15.2	15.3	17.8	17.5	17.2	17.1	15.8	17.2

[1] Data for 1994 are not directly comparable with data for 1993 and earlier years. For additional information, see "Revisions in the Current Population Survey Effective January 1994" in the February 1994 issue of *Employment and Earnings*.

[2] The population figures are not adjusted for seasonal variation; therefore, identical numbers appear in the unadjusted and seasonally adjusted columns.

NOTE: Seasonally adjusted data for 1994 have been revised.

HOUSEHOLD DATA

Table A-2. Employment status of the civilian population by race, sex, age, and Hispanic origin

(Numbers in thousands)

Employment status, race, sex, age, and Hispanic origin	Not seasonally adjusted			Seasonally adjusted[2]					
	Dec. 1993	Nov. 1994[1]	Dec. 1994	Dec. 1993	Aug. 1994[1]	Sept. 1994	Oct. 1994	Nov. 1994	Dec. 1994
WHITE									
Civilian noninstitutional population	164,516	166,072	166,175	164,516	165,698	165,832	165,954	166,072	166,175
Civilian labor force	109,576	111,703	111,385	110,016	111,186	111,381	111,555	111,637	111,715
Participation rate	66.6	67.3	67.0	66.9	67.1	67.2	67.2	67.2	67.2
Employed	103,733	106,655	106,427	103,807	105,401	105,740	106,010	106,242	106,362
Employment-population ratio	63.1	64.2	64.0	63.1	63.6	63.8	63.9	64.0	64.0
Unemployed	5,844	5,048	4,958	6,209	5,785	5,641	5,545	5,395	5,363
Unemployment rate	5.3	4.5	4.5	5.6	5.2	5.1	5.0	4.8	4.8
Men, 20 years and over									
Civilian labor force	57,087	57,744	57,730	57,280	57,387	57,478	57,615	57,726	57,836
Participation rate	77.1	77.4	77.4	77.4	77.2	77.2	77.3	77.4	77.5
Employed	54,102	55,441	55,334	54,283	54,734	54,926	55,061	55,242	55,384
Employment-population ratio	73.1	74.3	74.2	73.3	73.6	73.8	73.9	74.1	74.2
Unemployed	2,985	2,303	2,396	2,997	2,653	2,552	2,554	2,484	2,452
Unemployment rate	5.2	4.0	4.1	5.2	4.6	4.4	4.4	4.3	4.2
Women, 20 years and over									
Civilian labor force	46,977	47,975	47,507	46,872	47,403	47,737	47,614	47,631	47,440
Participation rate	58.8	59.8	59.2	58.7	59.2	59.6	59.4	59.4	59.1
Employed	44,834	45,992	45,747	44,554	45,204	45,560	45,535	45,569	45,475
Employment-population ratio	56.1	57.4	57.0	55.8	56.5	56.9	56.8	56.8	56.7
Unemployed	2,143	1,983	1,760	2,318	2,199	2,177	2,079	2,062	1,965
Unemployment rate	4.6	4.1	3.7	4.9	4.6	4.6	4.4	4.3	4.1
Both sexes, 16 to 19 years									
Civilian labor force	5,533	5,984	6,148	5,864	6,398	6,168	6,326	6,280	6,439
Participation rate	52.0	52.9	54.3	55.1	56.6	54.8	56.0	55.5	56.9
Employed	4,797	5,222	5,346	4,970	5,463	5,254	5,414	5,431	5,493
Employment-population ratio	45.1	46.2	47.2	46.7	48.4	46.5	47.9	48.0	48.5
Unemployed	736	762	802	894	933	912	912	849	946
Unemployment rate	13.3	12.7	13.0	15.2	14.6	14.8	14.4	13.5	14.7
Men	15.9	13.6	15.2	16.9	15.4	16.2	15.2	14.3	16.0
Women	10.6	11.8	10.8	13.4	13.7	13.3	13.5	12.6	13.2
BLACK									
Civilian noninstitutional population	22,504	23,023	23,052	22,504	22,917	22,955	22,990	23,023	23,052
Civilian labor force	13,935	14,566	14,470	14,011	14,429	14,477	14,649	14,578	14,541
Participation rate	61.9	63.3	62.8	62.3	63.0	63.1	63.7	63.3	63.1
Employed	12,406	13,080	13,154	12,397	12,795	12,927	13,022	13,054	13,119
Employment-population ratio	55.1	56.8	57.1	55.1	55.8	56.3	56.6	56.7	56.9
Unemployed	1,529	1,486	1,316	1,614	1,634	1,550	1,627	1,524	1,422
Unemployment rate	11.0	10.2	9.1	11.5	11.3	10.7	11.1	10.5	9.8
Men, 20 years and over									
Civilian labor force	6,434	6,703	6,723	6,469	6,570	6,637	6,706	6,702	6,722
Participation rate	70.6	72.6	72.7	70.9	71.5	72.1	72.7	72.6	72.7
Employed	5,793	6,097	6,199	5,787	5,898	5,989	6,069	6,085	6,165
Employment-population ratio	63.5	66.0	67.0	63.5	64.2	65.1	65.8	65.9	66.7
Unemployed	641	605	524	682	672	648	637	617	557
Unemployment rate	10.0	9.0	7.8	10.5	10.2	9.8	9.5	9.2	8.3
Women, 20 years and over									
Civilian labor force	6,824	7,041	7,001	6,801	7,012	7,001	7,033	7,012	7,002
Participation rate	60.5	60.9	60.5	60.3	60.9	60.7	60.9	60.7	60.5
Employed	6,171	6,417	6,443	6,143	6,356	6,368	6,384	6,390	6,420
Employment-population ratio	54.7	55.5	55.7	54.5	55.2	55.2	55.3	55.3	55.5
Unemployed	653	625	558	658	656	633	649	622	582
Unemployment rate	9.6	8.9	8.0	9.7	9.4	9.0	9.2	8.9	8.3
Both sexes, 16 to 19 years									
Civilian labor force	676	822	746	741	847	839	910	864	817
Participation rate	32.1	36.9	33.5	35.2	38.3	37.8	40.9	38.8	36.6
Employed	442	566	513	467	541	570	569	579	534
Employment-population ratio	21.0	25.4	23.0	22.2	24.5	25.7	25.6	26.0	23.9
Unemployed	234	256	234	274	306	269	341	285	283
Unemployment rate	34.6	31.1	31.3	37.0	36.1	32.1	37.5	33.0	34.6
Men	37.4	28.6	31.0	38.8	39.9	30.8	35.9	32.0	34.3
Women	32.0	33.8	31.7	35.2	31.9	33.4	39.1	34.1	35.0

See footnotes at end of table.

Table A-2. Employment status of the civilian population by race, sex, age, and Hispanic origin — Continued

(Numbers in thousands)

Employment status, race, sex, age, and Hispanic origin	Not seasonally adjusted			Seasonally adjusted[2]					
	Dec. 1993	Nov. 1994[1]	Dec. 1994	Dec. 1993	Aug. 1994[1]	Sept. 1994	Oct. 1994	Nov. 1994	Dec. 1994
HISPANIC ORIGIN									
Civilian noninstitutional population	16,014	18,339	18,385	16,014	18,193	18,244	18,291	18,339	18,385
Civilian labor force	10,550	12,215	12,078	10,625	12,002	11,997	12,222	12,324	12,224
Participation rate	65.9	66.6	65.7	66.3	66.0	65.8	66.8	67.2	66.5
Employed	9,483	11,160	11,005	9,513	10,786	10,806	11,074	11,236	11,105
Employment-population ratio	59.2	60.9	59.9	59.4	59.3	59.2	60.5	61.3	60.4
Unemployed	1,067	1,055	1,073	1,112	1,216	1,191	1,148	1,088	1,119
Unemployment rate	10.1	8.6	8.9	10.5	10.1	9.9	9.4	8.8	9.2

[1] Data for 1994 are not directly comparable with data for 1993 and earlier years. For additional information, see "Revisions in the Current Population Survey Effective January 1994" in the February 1994 issue of *Employment and Earnings*.

[2] The population figures are not adjusted for seasonal variation; therefore, identical numbers appear in the unadjusted and seasonally adjusted columns.

NOTE: Detail for the above race and Hispanic-origin groups will not sum to totals because data for the "other races" group are not presented and Hispanics are included in both the white and black population groups. Seasonally adjusted data for 1994 have been revised.

Table A-3. Selected employment indicators

(Numbers in thousands)

Category	Not seasonally adjusted			Seasonally adjusted					
	Dec. 1993	Nov. 1994[1]	Dec. 1994	Dec. 1993	Aug. 1994[1]	Sept. 1994	Oct. 1994	Nov. 1994	Dec. 1994
CHARACTERISTIC									
Total employed, 16 years and over	120,638	124,898	124,729	120,661	123,197	123,644	124,141	124,403	124,570
Married men, spouse present	41,089	41,672	41,775	40,951	41,487	41,557	41,511	41,530	41,608
Married women, spouse present	31,327	32,161	32,103	31,051	31,593	31,905	31,764	31,775	31,723
Women who maintain families	6,698	7,159	6,960	6,693	6,974	7,029	7,098	7,141	7,074
OCCUPATION									
Managerial and professional specialty	32,920	34,648	34,778	32,784	33,975	34,242	34,275	34,382	34,578
Technical, sales, and administrative support	37,425	37,779	38,143	37,243	37,373	37,635	37,669	37,767	37,797
Service occupations	16,717	16,754	16,631	16,734	16,866	16,749	17,062	16,893	16,704
Precision production, craft, and repair	13,373	13,868	13,685	13,445	13,454	13,452	13,467	13,615	13,677
Operators, fabricators, and laborers	17,269	18,245	18,069	17,209	17,975	18,023	18,122	18,058	18,030
Farming, forestry, and fishing	2,933	3,605	3,424	3,325	3,642	3,632	3,655	3,727	3,839
CLASS OF WORKER									
Agriculture:									
Wage and salary workers	1,611	1,768	1,660	1,724	1,728	1,712	1,764	1,767	1,738
Self-employed workers	1,154	1,664	1,583	1,269	1,654	1,630	1,652	1,677	1,714
Unpaid family workers	72	48	42	92	50	63	43	48	49
Nonagricultural industries:									
Wage and salary workers	108,552	112,315	112,389	108,247	110,578	111,100	111,686	111,770	111,960
Government	18,712	18,528	18,454	18,503	18,225	18,308	18,201	18,357	18,340
Private industries	89,839	93,788	93,935	89,744	92,351	92,794	93,485	93,413	93,620
Private households	1,056	964	1,004	1,104	881	903	935	999	1,023
Other industries	88,783	92,824	92,931	88,640	91,470	91,891	92,550	92,414	92,597
Self-employed workers	9,049	8,986	8,944	9,053	9,021	8,989	8,878	8,915	8,959
Unpaid family workers	199	115	111	217	131	134	131	120	121
PERSONS AT WORK PART TIME									
All industries:									
Part time for economic reasons	6,090	4,368	4,408	6,217	4,348	4,333	4,411	4,411	4,422
Slack work or business conditions	3,221	2,374	2,463	3,099	2,396	2,404	2,394	2,394	2,384
Could only find part-time work	2,656	1,688	1,621	2,828	1,618	1,697	1,791	1,736	1,734
Part time for noneconomic reasons	16,528	19,284	18,972	15,373	17,955	17,609	17,644	17,756	17,576
Nonagricultural industries:									
Part time for economic reasons	5,787	4,156	4,157	5,934	4,173	4,154	4,226	4,246	4,254
Slack work or business conditions	3,000	2,250	2,313	2,922	2,272	2,290	2,257	2,282	2,272
Could only find part-time work	2,585	1,641	1,584	2,739	1,583	1,648	1,756	1,689	1,690
Part time for noneconomic reasons	16,118	18,634	18,311	14,909	17,314	16,982	16,992	17,101	16,917

[1] Data for 1994 are not directly comparable with data for 1993 and earlier years. For additional information, see "Revisions in the Current Population Survey Effective January 1994" in the February 1994 issue of *Employment and Earnings*.

NOTE: Persons at work excludes employed persons who were absent from their jobs during the entire reference week for reasons such as vacation, illness, or industrial dispute. Part time for noneconomic reasons excludes persons who usually work full time but worked only 1 to 34 hours during the reference week for reasons such as holidays, illness, and bad weather. Seasonally adjusted data for 1994 have been revised.

Table A-4. Selected unemployment indicators, seasonally adjusted

(Numbers in thousands)

Category	Number of unemployed persons (in thousands)			Unemployment rates[2]					
	Dec. 1993	Nov. 1994[1]	Dec. 1994	Dec. 1993	Aug 1994[1]	Sept. 1994	Oct 1994	Nov 1994	Dec. 1994
CHARACTERISTIC									
Total, 16 years and over	8,237	7,315	7,155	6.4	6.0	5.8	5.7	5.6	5.4
Men, 20 years and over	3,877	3,294	3,169	5.8	5.3	5.1	5.0	4.9	4.7
Women, 20 years and over	3,152	2,855	2,688	5.7	5.3	5.2	5.0	5.0	4.7
Both sexes, 16 to 19 years	1,208	1,166	1,298	17.8	17.5	17.2	17.1	15.8	17.2
Married men, spouse present	1,873	1,393	1,358	3.9	3.5	3.4	3.3	3.2	3.2
Married women, spouse present	1,405	1,278	1,213	4.3	4.1	4.0	4.0	3.9	3.7
Women who maintain families	760	680	684	10.2	8.8	8.9	8.9	8.7	8.8
Full-time workers	6,760	5,987	5,677	6.4	6.0	5.8	5.8	5.6	5.3
Part-time workers	1,489	1,342	1,478	6.6	6.2	5.8	5.6	5.4	5.9
OCCUPATION[3]									
Managerial and professional specialty	952	849	805	2.8	2.6	2.5	2.5	2.4	2.3
Technical, sales, and administrative support	1,963	1,824	1,699	5.1	4.9	4.7	4.5	4.6	4.3
Precision production, craft, and repair	1,075	814	830	7.4	6.1	6.0	5.8	5.6	5.7
Operators, fabricators, and laborers	1,730	1,634	1,610	9.1	8.8	8.4	8.5	8.3	8.2
Farming, forestry, and fishing	316	303	323	8.7	8.6	8.2	8.4	7.5	7.8
INDUSTRY									
Nonagricultural private wage and salary workers	6,391	5,828	5,594	6.6	6.1	6.0	5.9	5.9	5.6
Goods-producing industries	2,138	1,753	1,734	7.9	6.5	6.5	6.4	6.3	6.2
Mining	51	31	28	6.9	5.0	5.1	4.7	4.5	3.9
Construction	765	674	682	12.7	10.7	10.7	10.7	10.7	10.9
Manufacturing	1,322	1,048	1,024	6.5	5.3	5.3	5.1	5.1	4.9
Durable goods	747	518	550	6.3	5.3	5.3	4.8	4.3	4.6
Nondurable goods	575	530	474	6.8	5.3	5.4	5.6	6.0	5.4
Service-producing industries	4,253	4,075	3,860	6.2	6.0	5.8	5.7	5.7	5.4
Transportation and public utilities	353	325	297	5.1	4.8	4.5	4.4	4.6	4.2
Wholesale and retail trade	1,843	1,815	1,729	7.4	7.4	7.0	7.2	7.0	6.7
Finance, insurance, and real estate	273	270	218	3.7	3.7	4.3	3.4	3.6	2.9
Services	1,784	1,665	1,616	5.9	5.7	5.5	5.3	5.4	5.2
Government workers	598	507	587	3.1	3.6	3.2	3.2	2.7	3.1
Agricultural wage and salary workers	220	204	217	11.3	11.1	11.1	10.3	10.4	11.1

[1] Data for 1994 are not directly comparable with data for 1993 and earlier years. For additional information, see "Revisions in the Current Population Survey Effective January 1994" in the February 1994 issue of *Employment and Earnings*.

[2] Unemployment as a percent of the civilian labor force.

[3] Seasonally adjusted unemployment data for service occupations are not available because the seasonal components are small relative to the trend-cycle and/or irregular components and consequently cannot be separated with sufficient precision.

NOTE: Seasonally adjusted data for 1994 have been revised.

Table A-5. Duration of unemployment

(Numbers in thousands)

Duration	Not seasonally adjusted			Seasonally adjusted					
	Dec. 1993	Nov. 1994[1]	Dec. 1994	Dec. 1993	Aug 1994[1]	Sept. 1994	Oct 1994	Nov 1994	Dec 1994
NUMBER OF UNEMPLOYED									
Less than 5 weeks	2,784	2,467	2,249	3,063	2,655	2,675	2,434	2,599	2,587
5 to 14 weeks	2,297	2,063	2,156	2,247	2,572	2,294	2,256	2,163	2,149
15 weeks and over	2,703	2,443	2,285	2,864	2,773	2,768	2,934	2,661	2,456
15 to 26 weeks	1,071	1,068	1,019	1,150	1,198	1,213	1,344	1,187	1,088
27 weeks and over	1,632	1,374	1,266	1,714	1,575	1,555	1,590	1,474	1,368
Average (mean) duration, in weeks	18.4	17.9	17.7	18.2	18.9	18.8	19.3	18.2	17.8
Median duration, in weeks	8.4	8.7	8.7	8.2	9.2	9.5	10.1	9.1	8.7
PERCENT DISTRIBUTION									
Total unemployed	100.0	100.0	100.0	100.0	100.0	100.0	100.0	100.0	100.0
Less than 5 weeks	35.8	35.4	33.6	37.5	33.2	34.6	31.9	35.0	36.0
5 to 14 weeks	29.6	29.6	32.2	27.5	32.1	29.6	29.6	29.1	29.9
15 weeks and over	34.8	35.0	34.2	35.0	34.7	35.8	38.5	35.8	34.1
15 to 26 weeks	13.8	15.3	15.2	14.1	15.0	15.7	17.6	16.0	15.1
27 weeks and over	21.0	19.7	18.9	21.0	19.7	20.1	20.9	19.9	19.0

[1] Data for 1994 are not directly comparable with data for 1993 and earlier years. For additional information, see "Revisions in the Current Population Survey Effective January 1994" in the February 1994 issue of *Employment and Earnings*.

NOTE: Seasonally adjusted data for 1994 have been revised.

HOUSEHOLD DATA

Table A-6. Reason for unemployment

(Numbers in thousands)

Reason	Not seasonally adjusted			Seasonally adjusted					
	Dec. 1993	Nov. 1994[1]	Dec. 1994	Dec. 1993	Aug. 1994[1]	Sept. 1994	Oct. 1994	Nov. 1994	Dec. 1994
NUMBER OF UNEMPLOYED									
Job losers and persons who completed temporary jobs	4,492	3,366	3,514	4,442	3,708	3,574	3,513	3,495	3,442
On temporary layoff	1,145	803	1,050	1,060	1,012	824	848	881	930
Not on temporary layoff	3,348	2,563	2,464	3,382	2,694	2,750	2,665	2,614	2,512
Permanent job losers	(2)	1,801	1,699	(2)	(2)	(2)	(2)	(2)	(2)
Persons who completed temporary jobs	(2)	762	765	(2)	(2)	(2)	(2)	(2)	(2)
Job leavers	834	714	616	932	786	874	755	710	704
Reentrants	1,783	2,407	2,180	2,018	2,758	2,620	2,626	2,575	2,525
New entrants	655	486	380	797	621	600	614	578	555
PERCENT DISTRIBUTION									
Total unemployed	100.0	100.0	100.0	100.0	100.0	100.0	100.0	100.0	100.0
Job losers and persons who completed temporary jobs	57.9	48.3	52.5	54.2	47.1	46.6	46.8	47.5	47.6
On temporary layoff	14.7	11.5	15.7	12.9	12.9	10.7	11.3	12.0	12.9
Not on temporary layoff	43.1	36.8	36.8	41.3	34.2	35.9	35.5	35.5	34.8
Job leavers	10.7	10.2	9.2	11.4	10.0	11.4	10.1	9.6	9.7
Reentrants	23.0	34.5	32.6	24.6	35.0	34.2	35.0	35.0	34.9
New entrants	8.4	7.0	5.7	9.7	7.9	7.8	8.2	7.9	7.7
UNEMPLOYED AS A PERCENT OF THE CIVILIAN LABOR FORCE									
Job losers and persons who completed temporary jobs	3.5	2.6	2.7	3.4	2.8	2.7	2.7	2.7	2.6
Job leavers	.6	.5	.5	.7	.6	.7	.6	.5	.5
Reentrants	1.4	1.8	1.7	1.6	2.1	2.0	2.0	2.0	1.9
New entrants	.5	.4	.3	.6	.5	.5	.5	.4	.4

[1] Data for 1994 are not directly comparable with data for 1993 and earlier years. For additional information, see "Revisions in the Current Population Survey Effective January 1994" in the February 1994 issue of *Employment and Earnings*.

[2] Not available.

NOTE: Seasonally adjusted data for 1994 have been revised.

Table A-7. Unemployed persons by sex and age, seasonally adjusted

Age and sex	Number of unemployed persons (in thousands)			Unemployment rates[2]					
	Dec. 1993	Nov. 1994[1]	Dec. 1994	Dec. 1993	Aug. 1994[1]	Sept. 1994	Oct. 1994	Nov. 1994	Dec. 1994
Total, 16 years and over	8,237	7,315	7,155	6.4	6.0	5.8	5.7	5.6	5.4
16 to 24 years	2,480	2,450	2,513	12.3	12.6	12.1	11.8	11.4	11.6
16 to 19 years	1,208	1,166	1,298	17.8	17.5	17.2	17.1	15.8	17.2
16 to 17 years	527	539	573	19.0	19.9	18.8	17.8	17.2	18.1
18 to 19 years	689	624	728	17.1	15.6	16.0	16.8	14.7	16.6
20 to 24 years	1,272	1,284	1,215	9.5	9.9	9.4	9.0	9.1	8.6
25 years and over	5,750	4,926	4,717	5.3	4.7	4.6	4.5	4.5	4.3
25 to 54 years	5,108	4,297	4,130	5.5	4.8	4.8	4.7	4.5	4.4
55 years and over	657	615	539	4.2	4.2	3.8	3.9	3.9	3.5
Men, 16 years and over	4,554	3,924	3,898	6.5	6.1	5.8	5.7	5.5	5.5
16 to 24 years	1,389	1,348	1,411	13.2	13.3	12.6	12.4	11.8	12.2
16 to 19 years	677	630	727	19.4	18.8	18.5	18.1	16.5	18.5
16 to 17 years	286	271	313	19.9	20.7	19.4	18.2	16.5	18.8
18 to 19 years	390	361	411	18.9	17.1	17.5	18.1	16.5	18.2
20 to 24 years	712	718	684	10.1	10.5	9.5	9.4	9.5	9.0
25 years and over	3,171	2,626	2,551	5.4	4.7	4.5	4.5	4.4	4.3
25 to 54 years	2,774	2,249	2,217	5.5	4.8	4.6	4.6	4.4	4.3
55 years and over	411	349	308	4.7	4.2	3.9	4.1	4.0	3.5
Women, 16 years and over	3,683	3,391	3,259	6.2	6.0	5.8	5.7	5.6	5.4
16 to 24 years	1,091	1,104	1,102	11.3	11.7	11.6	11.2	10.9	10.9
16 to 19 years	531	536	571	16.1	16.1	15.9	16.0	15.0	15.8
16 to 17 years	241	268	260	18.1	19.0	18.2	17.4	17.9	17.4
18 to 19 years	299	263	317	15.1	14.0	14.2	15.4	12.8	14.9
20 to 24 years	560	568	531	8.8	9.3	9.3	8.6	8.7	8.1
25 years and over	2,579	2,300	2,166	5.2	4.8	4.7	4.6	4.6	4.3
25 to 54 years	2,332	2,048	1,913	5.5	4.9	5.0	4.8	4.7	4.4
55 years and over	248	266	233	3.6	4.1	3.6	3.7	3.8	3.4

[1] Data for 1994 are not directly comparable with data for 1993 and earlier years. For additional information, see "Revisions in the Current Population Survey Effective January 1994" in the February 1994 issue of *Employment and Earnings*.

[2] Unemployment as a percent of the civilian labor force.

NOTE: Seasonally adjusted data for 1994 have been revised.

Table A-8. Persons not in the labor force and multiple jobholders by sex, not seasonally adjusted

(Numbers in thousands)

Category	December 1994		
	Total	Men	Women
NOT IN THE LABOR FORCE			
Total not in the labor force	66,347	23,792	42,555
Persons who currently want a job	5,604	2,260	3,344
Searched for work and available to work now[1]	1,810	829	982
Reason not currently looking:			
Discouragement over job prospects[2]	445	265	180
Reasons other than discouragement[3]	1,366	564	802
MULTIPLE JOBHOLDERS			
Total multiple jobholders[4]	7,539	4,032	3,507
Percent of total employed	6.0	6.0	6.1
Primary job full time, secondary job part time	4,388	2,618	1,748
Primary and secondary jobs both part time	1,751	582	1,170
Primary and secondary jobs both full time	232	144	88
Hours vary on primary or secondary job	1,149	671	478

[1] Data refer to persons who have searched for work during the prior 12 months and were available to take a job during the reference week.

[2] Includes thinks no work available, could not find work, lacks schooling or training, employer thinks too young or old, and other types of discrimination.

[3] Includes those who did not actively look for work in the prior 4 weeks for such reasons as child-care and transportation problems, as well as a small number for which reason for nonparticipation was not determined.

[4] Includes persons who work part time on their primary job and full time on their secondary job(s), not shown separately.

HOUSEHOLD DATA

Table A-9. Employment status of the civilian population for 11 large states

(Numbers in thousands)

State and employment status	Not seasonally adjusted[1]			Seasonally adjusted[3]					
	Dec. 1993	Nov. 1994[2]	Dec. 1994	Dec. 1993	Aug. 1994[2]	Sept. 1994	Oct. 1994	Nov. 1994	Dec. 1994
California									
Civilian noninstitutional population	23,367	23,515	23,527	23,367	23,467	23,484	23,500	23,515	23,527
Civilian labor force	15,202	15,454	15,340	15,216	15,390	15,463	15,608	15,497	15,384
Employed	13,937	14,292	14,261	13,884	14,023	14,172	14,411	14,299	14,243
Unemployed	1,265	1,162	1,078	1,332	1,367	1,290	1,197	1,198	1,141
Unemployment rate	8.3	7.5	7.0	8.8	8.9	8.3	7.7	7.7	7.4
Florida									
Civilian noninstitutional population	10,756	10,886	10,897	10,756	10,847	10,861	10,873	10,886	10,897
Civilian labor force	6,697	6,903	6,849	6,742	6,718	6,843	6,829	6,928	6,899
Employed	6,292	6,475	6,479	6,277	6,344	6,386	6,384	6,455	6,462
Unemployed	405	427	370	464	374	457	445	473	436
Unemployment rate	6.0	6.2	5.4	6.9	5.6	6.7	6.5	6.8	6.3
Illinois									
Civilian noninstitutional population	8,857	8,906	8,910	8,857	8,889	8,895	8,901	8,906	8,910
Civilian labor force	6,043	6,007	5,985	6,033	5,986	5,952	6,050	6,011	5,968
Employed	5,689	5,738	5,732	5,675	5,646	5,612	5,672	5,713	5,716
Unemployed	353	270	253	358	340	340	378	298	252
Unemployment rate	5.8	4.5	4.2	5.9	5.7	5.7	6.3	5.0	4.2
Massachusetts									
Civilian noninstitutional population	4,668	4,668	4,668	4,666	4,665	4,667	4,667	4,668	4,668
Civilian labor force	3,159	3,159	3,180	3,162	3,172	3,181	3,183	3,164	3,179
Employed	2,976	2,994	3,013	2,966	2,984	3,014	2,979	2,990	2,999
Unemployed	183	165	167	196	188	167	205	174	180
Unemployment rate	5.8	5.2	5.2	6.2	5.9	5.2	6.4	5.5	5.7
Michigan									
Civilian noninstitutional population	7,150	7,183	7,186	7,150	7,172	7,176	7,180	7,183	7,186
Civilian labor force	4,749	4,760	4,731	4,748	4,744	4,810	4,817	4,760	4,733
Employed	4,426	4,561	4,537	4,399	4,447	4,545	4,570	4,540	4,520
Unemployed	323	200	195	349	297	265	247	220	213
Unemployment rate	6.8	4.2	4.1	7.3	6.3	5.5	5.1	4.6	4.5
New Jersey									
Civilian noninstitutional population	6,121	6,147	6,149	6,121	6,138	6,142	6,144	6,147	6,149
Civilian labor force	4,036	4,052	4,069	4,019	4,099	4,098	4,107	4,055	4,059
Employed	3,765	3,801	3,835	3,737	3,852	3,824	3,830	3,789	3,811
Unemployed	271	251	235	282	246	274	277	266	248
Unemployment rate	6.7	6.2	5.8	7.0	6.0	6.7	6.7	6.6	6.1
New York									
Civilian noninstitutional population	14,052	14,080	14,082	14,052	14,067	14,073	14,077	14,080	14,082
Civilian labor force	8,544	8,545	8,571	8,597	8,633	8,591	8,609	8,581	8,629
Employed	7,906	8,040	8,115	7,943	8,035	8,058	8,048	8,043	8,160
Unemployed	638	505	455	654	598	533	561	538	469
Unemployment rate	7.5	5.9	5.3	7.6	6.9	6.2	6.5	6.3	5.4

See footnotes at end of table.

HOUSEHOLD DATA

Table A-9. Employment status of the civilian population for 11 large states — Continued

(Numbers in thousands)

State and employment status	Not seasonally adjusted[1]			Seasonally adjusted[3]					
	Dec. 1993	Nov. 1994[2]	Dec. 1994	Dec. 1993	Aug 1994[2]	Sept. 1994	Oct 1994	Nov 1994	Dec. 1994
North Carolina									
Civilian noninstitutional population	5,328	5,401	5,408	5,328	5,379	5,387	5,394	5,401	5,408
Civilian labor force	3,544	3,667	3,660	3,565	3,613	3,638	3,624	3,645	3,682
Employed	3,410	3,524	3,553	3,417	3,424	3,452	3,443	3,497	3,560
Unemployed	134	143	108	148	189	186	180	148	122
Unemployment rate	3.8	3.9	2.9	4.1	5.2	5.1	5.0	4.1	3.3
Ohio									
Civilian noninstitutional population	8,416	8,450	8,453	8,416	8,438	8,443	8,446	8,450	8,453
Civilian labor force	5,514	5,572	5,556	5,551	5,437	5,520	5,557	5,598	5,593
Employed	5,175	5,338	5,320	5,203	5,143	5,217	5,282	5,336	5,352
Unemployed	339	234	235	348	294	303	274	262	241
Unemployment rate	6.1	4.2	4.2	6.3	5.4	5.5	4.9	4.7	4.3
Pennsylvania									
Civilian noninstitutional population	9,297	9,318	9,320	9,297	9,309	9,313	9,316	9,318	9,320
Civilian labor force	5,870	5,753	5,803	5,890	5,867	5,797	5,772	5,699	5,821
Employed	5,531	5,429	5,494	5,513	5,499	5,408	5,428	5,360	5,476
Unemployed	339	324	309	376	369	389	344	339	345
Unemployment rate	5.8	5.6	5.3	6.4	6.3	6.7	6.0	5.9	5.9
Texas									
Civilian noninstitutional population	13,421	13,652	13,673	13,421	13,585	13,608	13,631	13,652	13,673
Civilian labor force	9,271	9,498	9,421	9,301	9,416	9,334	9,398	9,476	9,441
Employed	8,686	8,967	8,879	8,691	8,791	8,751	8,842	8,956	8,873
Unemployed	585	531	542	611	626	583	555	520	567
Unemployment rate	6.3	5.6	5.8	6.6	6.6	6.2	5.9	5.5	6.0

[1] These are the official Bureau of Labor Statistics' estimates used in the administration of Federal fund allocation programs.

[2] Data for 1994 are not directly comparable with those for 1993 and earlier years. For additional information, see "Revisions in the Current Population Survey Effective January 1994" in the February 1994 issue of *Employment and Earnings*.

[3] The population figures are not adjusted for seasonal variation; therefore, identical numbers appear in the unadjusted and the seasonally adjusted columns.

NOTE: Revised seasonal adjustment factors are not yet available for State data. The seasonally adjusted series for 1994 will be revised with the release of January 1995 data on February 3.

Table B-1. Employees on nonfarm payrolls by industry

(In thousands)

Industry	Not seasonally adjusted				Seasonally adjusted					
	Dec. 1993	Oct. 1994	Nov. 1994p	Dec. 1994p	Dec. 1993	Aug. 1994	Sept. 1994	Oct. 1994	Nov. 1994p	Dec. 1994p
Total	112,374	115,266	115,823	115,858	111,610	113,914	114,186	114,348	114,836	115,092
Total private	93,135	95,880	96,202	96,388	92,692	94,827	95,035	95,228	95,642	95,928
Goods-producing industries	23,226	24,086	24,020	23,790	23,298	23,640	23,673	23,715	23,825	23,871
Mining	619	607	603	598	618	603	605	599	597	595
Metal mining	50.5	51.3	51.5	51.4	51	52	51	51	52	52
Coal mining	114.5	112.6	112.7	112.2	(1)	(1)	(1)	(1)	(1)	(1)
Oil and gas extraction	355.4	338.5	336.1	332.8	351	336	341	335	332	329
Nonmetallic minerals, except fuels	98.4	104.5	103.1	99.8	101	101	101	101	101	102
Construction	4,656	5,236	5,170	4,953	4,738	4,942	4,972	4,974	5,047	5,041
General building contractors	1,132.2	1,222.3	1,217.3	1,199.3	1,138	1,166	1,172	1,180	1,197	1,205
Heavy construction, except building	672.5	794.4	759.2	676.0	710	725	727	716	725	715
Special trade contractors	2,852.9	3,219.3	3,193.4	3,077.4	2,890	3,051	3,073	3,078	3,125	3,121
Manufacturing	17,949	18,243	18,247	18,241	17,942	18,095	18,098	18,142	18,181	18,235
Production workers	12,288	12,620	12,626	12,623	12,292	12,478	12,485	12,527	12,570	12,630
Durable goods	10,169	10,373	10,412	10,424	10,153	10,290	10,308	10,335	10,373	10,405
Production workers	6,851	7,086	7,123	7,136	6,843	7,007	7,021	7,054	7,090	7,129
Lumber and wood products	711.8	745.5	744.8	740.4	716	734	735	737	743	744
Furniture and fixtures	491.7	502.8	503.4	502.2	489	496	498	497	500	500
Stone, clay, and glass products	513.8	542.5	540.9	533.7	518	531	531	533	536	539
Primary metal industries	678.8	696.8	699.7	702.5	678	686	690	695	699	701
Blast furnaces and basic steel products	237.8	234.3	234.6	235.3	237	232	233	235	235	234
Fabricated metal products	1,343.1	1,389.2	1,396.6	1,400.2	1,338	1,373	1,373	1,381	1,388	1,398
Industrial machinery and equipment	1,919.8	1,951.4	1,960.9	1,967.2	1,918	1,952	1,956	1,957	1,963	1,965
Electronic and other electrical equipment	1,528.7	1,570.3	1,580.6	1,587.4	1,524	1,561	1,567	1,567	1,574	1,583
Transportation equipment	1,734.1	1,739.6	1,749.9	1,757.9	1,724	1,727	1,731	1,741	1,741	1,746
Motor vehicles and equipment	860.1	907.8	916.1	923.8	853	893	898	909	912	915
Aircraft and parts	509.8	467.5	466.3	467.2	507	472	468	467	464	464
Instruments and related products	874.1	845.5	846.5	847.1	873	850	848	845	846	846
Miscellaneous manufacturing	373.4	389.2	388.3	381.9	375	380	379	382	383	383
Nondurable goods	7,780	7,870	7,835	7,817	7,789	7,805	7,790	7,807	7,808	7,830
Production workers	5,437	5,534	5,503	5,487	5,449	5,471	5,464	5,473	5,480	5,501
Food and kindred products	1,655.1	1,706.4	1,677.2	1,659.3	1,671	1,666	1,661	1,662	1,669	1,674
Tobacco products	44.7	40.9	39.2	40.8	42	40	38	39	38	38
Textile mill products	670.4	674.5	674.8	673.0	671	672	669	672	673	674
Apparel and other textile products	958.5	964.6	955.2	944.3	959	958	957	956	948	946
Paper and allied products	685.1	684.3	685.5	686.1	685	683	680	684	685	686
Printing and publishing	1,523.1	1,535.5	1,541.3	1,550.7	1,514	1,535	1,533	1,537	1,537	1,543
Chemicals and allied products	1,069.2	1,047.5	1,045.1	1,047.6	1,070	1,050	1,049	1,049	1,046	1,049
Petroleum and coal products	146.8	151.0	149.1	147.3	149	149	149	149	148	150
Rubber and misc. plastics products	910.3	950.5	953.4	954.7	911	938	941	946	951	956
Leather and leather products	116.9	114.4	114.3	113.6	117	114	113	113	113	114
Service-producing industries	89,148	91,180	91,803	92,068	88,312	90,274	90,513	90,633	91,011	91,221
Transportation and public utilities	5,847	5,926	5,926	5,961	5,792	5,866	5,865	5,867	5,881	5,906
Transportation	3,668	3,751	3,750	3,786	3,611	3,691	3,694	3,694	3,705	3,729
Railroad transportation	246.8	247.1	243.7	240.3	248	241	245	245	244	242
Local and interurban passenger transit	391.5	409.4	409.2	412.3	376	397	390	390	392	397
Trucking and warehousing	1,750.5	1,804.5	1,810.1	1,840.4	1,704	1,772	1,775	1,773	1,782	1,794
Water transportation	162.8	167.3	162.3	161.7	165	165	167	166	164	164
Transportation by air	740.3	731.5	732.2	738.6	741	729	729	730	731	737
Pipelines, except natural gas	18.0	17.8	17.7	17.4	18	18	18	18	18	17
Transportation services	357.8	373.2	374.6	377.4	359	369	370	372	374	378
Communications and public utilities	2,179	2,175	2,176	2,175	2,181	2,175	2,171	2,173	2,176	2,177
Communications	1,247.8	1,262.4	1,265.3	1,266.2	1,246	1,261	1,257	1,260	1,262	1,265
Electric, gas, and sanitary services	930.9	912.2	910.5	908.4	935	914	914	913	914	912
Wholesale trade	5,977	6,127	6,135	6,127	5,976	6,079	6,095	6,106	6,116	6,127
Durable goods	3,420	3,484	3,495	3,503	3,419	3,471	3,476	3,484	3,492	3,503
Nondurable goods	2,557	2,643	2,640	2,624	2,557	2,608	2,619	2,622	2,624	2,624

See footnotes at end of table.

ESTABLISHMENT DATA

Table B-1. Employees on nonfarm payrolls by industry — Continued

(In thousands)

Industry	Not seasonally adjusted				Seasonally adjusted					
	Dec. 1993	Oct. 1994	Nov. 1994p	Dec. 1994p	Dec. 1993	Aug. 1994	Sept. 1994	Oct. 1994	Nov. 1994p	Dec. 1994p
Retail trade	20,486	20,555	20,913	21,288	19,931	20,406	20,470	20,523	20,619	20,710
Building materials and garden supplies	792.4	855.6	853.1	853.9	803	844	848	852	859	866
General merchandise stores	2,703.3	2,533.8	2,709.9	2,787.9	2,446	2,476	2,484	2,508	2,537	2,521
Food stores	3,287.5	3,282.1	3,293.7	3,335.2	3,214	3,254	3,248	3,252	3,264	3,283
Automotive dealers and service stations	2,081.7	2,189.2	2,191.9	2,191.7	2,074	2,159	2,171	2,180	2,194	2,205
Apparel and accessory stores	1,265.5	1,149.6	1,197.0	1,261.2	1,154	1,148	1,154	1,158	1,153	1,151
Furniture and home furnishings stores	885.1	923.1	954.9	981.5	852	905	914	925	936	944
Eating and drinking places	6,871.2	7,093.6	7,094.0	7,150.6	6,917	7,105	7,111	7,115	7,144	7,208
Miscellaneous retail establishments	2,638.8	2,547.5	2,618.0	2,704.4	2,471	2,514	2,540	2,535	2,532	2,532
Finance, insurance, and real estate	6,757	6,769	6,766	6,779	6,769	6,801	6,794	6,786	6,790	6,793
Finance	3,249	3,235	3,239	3,247	3,250	3,259	3,251	3,246	3,247	3,248
Depository institutions	2,063.6	2,028.6	2,029.6	2,035.4	2,064	2,040	2,036	2,037	2,036	2,035
Nondepository institutions	471.9	464.6	461.4	459.8	472	476	472	466	463	460
Security and commodity brokers	484.6	506.8	510.3	511.7	486	508	508	507	511	513
Holding and other investment offices	228.6	235.3	237.3	240.3	228	235	235	236	237	240
Insurance	2,191	2,171	2,170	2,173	2,190	2,180	2,178	2,177	2,174	2,173
Insurance carriers	1,527.7	1,504.2	1,502.3	1,503.8	1,527	1,515	1,512	1,509	1,505	1,504
Insurance agents, brokers, and service	662.9	666.3	667.4	669.4	663	665	666	668	669	669
Real estate	1,317	1,363	1,357	1,359	1,329	1,362	1,365	1,363	1,369	1,372
Services[2]	30,842	32,417	32,442	32,443	30,928	32,036	32,138	32,231	32,411	32,521
Agricultural services	490.7	583.6	564.0	529.3	538	559	561	564	569	577
Hotels and other lodging places	1,544.2	1,590.8	1,539.5	1,534.4	1,599	1,619	1,609	1,594	1,587	1,592
Personal services	1,130.6	1,114.1	1,113.0	1,122.2	1,140	1,139	1,138	1,138	1,136	1,130
Business services	6,107.0	6,778.8	6,824.6	6,831.0	6,062	6,538	6,593	6,628	6,730	6,784
Personnel supply services	2,141.4	2,565.5	2,566.2	2,561.3	2,103	2,388	2,418	2,425	2,491	2,516
Auto repair, services, and parking	980.2	1,075.4	1,080.9	1,083.8	986	1,058	1,065	1,073	1,082	1,090
Miscellaneous repair services	368.2	387.5	387.3	385.7	370	382	382	384	387	388
Motion pictures	438.1	506.8	530.2	541.6	432	493	502	515	531	533
Amusement and recreation services	1,145.8	1,205.0	1,146.3	1,144.6	1,254	1,266	1,254	1,272	1,272	1,255
Health services	8,897.5	9,105.9	9,122.8	9,153.7	8,890	9,076	9,084	9,108	9,114	9,145
Hospitals	3,785.2	3,786.7	3,787.5	3,788.4	3,787	3,790	3,791	3,790	3,788	3,792
Legal services	932.1	942.4	946.7	948.2	934	942	946	945	949	950
Educational services	1,804.1	1,881.1	1,914.4	1,879.8	1,708	1,747	1,761	1,761	1,773	1,780
Social services	2,165.5	2,307.0	2,328.1	2,337.7	2,154	2,285	2,298	2,300	2,314	2,328
Museums and botanical and zoological gardens	75.0	81.0	77.8	77.9	77	80	79	79	80	80
Membership organizations	2,029.8	2,053.2	2,052.2	2,052.4	2,040	2,056	2,062	2,064	2,065	2,063
Engineering and management services	2,558.4	2,630.1	2,639.3	2,645.5	2,567	2,621	2,632	2,635	2,647	2,653
Services, nec	40.5	41.0	41.1	41.2	(1)	(1)	(1)	(1)	(1)	(1)
Government	19,239	19,386	19,621	19,492	18,918	19,087	19,151	19,120	19,194	19,164
Federal	2,918	2,844	2,836	2,870	2,915	2,858	2,863	2,858	2,853	2,867
State	4,597	4,698	4,723	4,685	4,511	4,585	4,593	4,581	4,590	4,596
Education	1,955.1	2,003.0	2,038.8	2,001.5	1,841	1,886	1,890	1,875	1,881	1,885
Other State government	2,642.0	2,692.7	2,684.2	2,683.8	2,670	2,699	2,703	2,708	2,709	2,711
Local	11,724	11,846	12,062	11,937	11,492	11,644	11,695	11,681	11,751	11,701
Education	6,717.2	6,774.0	6,883.6	6,871.7	6,390	6,536	6,547	6,532	6,531	6,538
Other local government	5,007.2	5,071.7	5,178.0	5,065.0	5,102	5,108	5,148	5,149	5,220	5,163

[1] These series are not published seasonally adjusted since the seasonal component is small relative to the trend-cycle and/or irregular components and consequently cannot be separated with sufficient precision.

[2] Includes other industries, not shown separately.

p = preliminary.

ESTABLISHMENT DATA

Table B-2. Average weekly hours of production or nonsupervisory workers[1] on private nonfarm payrolls by industry

Industry	Not seasonally adjusted				Seasonally adjusted					
	Dec. 1993	Oct. 1994	Nov. 1994p	Dec. 1994p	Dec. 1993	Aug. 1994	Sept. 1994	Oct. 1994	Nov. 1994p	Dec. 1994p
Total private	34.7	34.9	34.6	34.8	34.5	34.4	34.8	34.9	34.8	34.6
Mining	44.8	45.2	45.5	45.0	44.1	44.7	45.0	44.8	45.1	44.6
Construction	38.3	39.5	38.5	38.7	(2)	(2)	(2)	(2)	(2)	(2)
Manufacturing	42.4	42.3	42.5	43.0	41.7	42.0	42.0	42.1	42.2	42.2
Overtime hours	4.8	4.9	5.0	5.2	4.4	4.6	4.7	4.7	4.7	4.8
Durable goods	43.4	43.1	43.3	43.9	42.5	42.8	42.8	42.9	43.0	43.1
Overtime hours	5.2	5.2	5.3	5.7	4.7	5.0	5.0	5.0	5.0	5.2
Lumber and wood products	41.6	41.6	41.2	41.7	41.2	41.2	40.9	41.4	41.1	41.3
Furniture and fixtures	41.4	41.2	41.0	41.6	40.2	40.4	40.7	40.8	40.7	40.4
Stone, clay, and glass products	42.9	44.2	43.7	43.4	43.1	43.4	43.8	43.5	43.4	43.6
Primary metal industries	44.7	44.7	45.2	45.7	44.2	44.7	44.9	44.9	45.1	45.2
Blast furnaces and basic steel products	44.8	45.2	45.5	46.1	44.2	45.0	45.3	45.4	45.5	45.7
Fabricated metal products	43.5	43.1	43.6	44.1	42.5	42.8	43.0	42.8	43.2	43.2
Industrial machinery and equipment	44.4	43.7	44.0	44.8	43.3	43.4	43.7	43.7	43.9	43.7
Electronic and other electrical equipment	43.0	42.3	42.6	43.4	41.9	42.3	42.0	42.3	42.1	42.3
Transportation equipment	44.9	44.5	44.9	46.0	44.1	44.4	44.2	44.2	44.7	45.1
Motor vehicles and equipment	46.8	45.9	46.5	47.3	46.1	45.9	45.8	45.6	46.6	46.6
Instruments and related products	42.1	41.7	42.1	42.7	41.2	41.8	41.7	41.8	41.8	41.6
Miscellaneous manufacturing	40.8	40.6	40.7	40.4	39.9	39.9	39.9	40.0	39.9	39.8
Nondurable goods	41.2	41.3	41.5	41.7	40.8	40.9	41.0	41.1	41.0	41.1
Overtime hours	4.2	4.6	4.5	4.5	4.0	4.2	4.3	4.3	4.3	4.3
Food and kindred products	41.3	41.9	42.2	42.1	40.7	41.3	41.3	41.4	41.5	41.5
Tobacco products	37.4	41.8	39.8	41.4	(2)	(2)	(2)	(2)	(2)	(2)
Textile mill products	42.2	42.0	41.9	42.3	41.8	41.5	41.5	41.9	41.5	41.9
Apparel and other textile products	37.8	38.0	38.0	38.2	37.1	37.7	37.6	37.7	37.6	37.8
Paper and allied products	44.5	44.3	44.3	44.5	43.7	44.1	43.9	44.1	43.9	43.7
Printing and publishing	38.9	38.9	39.1	39.2	38.3	38.5	38.7	38.7	38.7	38.6
Chemicals and allied products	44.0	43.4	43.8	44.0	43.1	43.2	43.1	43.5	43.5	43.2
Petroleum and coal products	43.4	45.1	44.8	44.8	(2)	(2)	(2)	(2)	(2)	(2)
Rubber and misc. plastics products	42.8	42.3	42.6	43.1	42.0	42.2	42.4	42.3	42.3	42.5
Leather and leather products	39.0	39.1	38.9	38.7	38.5	38.8	38.8	39.1	38.8	38.2
Transportation and public utilities	39.8	40.2	39.8	40.0	39.7	39.6	39.9	40.1	39.8	39.9
Wholesale trade	38.3	38.7	38.4	38.4	38.1	38.1	38.2	38.6	38.4	38.2
Retail trade	29.3	29.1	28.7	29.2	28.8	28.9	28.8	29.2	28.9	28.8
Finance, insurance, and real estate	35.7	36.2	35.6	35.7	(2)	(2)	(2)	(2)	(2)	(2)
Services	32.4	32.8	32.4	32.5	32.4	32.2	32.5	32.8	32.4	32.5

[1] Data relate to production workers in mining and manufacturing; construction workers in construction; and nonsupervisory workers in transportation and public utilities; wholesale and retail trade; finance, insurance, and real estate; and services. These groups account for approximately four-fifths of the total employees on private nonfarm payrolls.

[2] These series are not published seasonally adjusted since the seasonal component is small relative to the trend-cycle and/or irregular components and consequently cannot be separated with sufficient precision.

p = preliminary.

 ESTABLISHMENT DATA

Table B-3. Average hourly and weekly earnings of production or nonsupervisory workers[1] on private nonfarm payrolls by industry

Industry	Average hourly earnings				Average weekly earnings			
	Dec. 1993	Oct. 1994	Nov. 1994p	Dec. 1994p	Dec. 1993	Oct. 1994	Nov. 1994p	Dec. 1994p
Total private	$10.97	$11.26	$11.25	$11.28	$380.66	$392.97	$389.25	$392.54
Seasonally adjusted	10.96	11.25	11.23	11.26	378.12	392.63	388.56	389.60
Mining	14.67	14.91	14.95	15.03	654.28	673.93	680.23	676.35
Construction	14.46	15.03	14.84	14.78	553.82	593.69	571.34	571.99
Manufacturing	12.00	12.10	12.17	12.28	508.80	511.83	517.23	528.04
Durable goods	12.62	12.70	12.77	12.90	547.71	547.37	552.94	566.31
Lumber and wood products	9.72	9.95	9.91	9.98	404.35	413.92	408.29	416.17
Furniture and fixtures	9.44	9.70	9.69	9.79	390.82	399.64	397.29	407.26
Stone, clay, and glass products	11.95	12.21	12.21	12.23	512.66	539.68	533.58	530.78
Primary metal industries	14.26	14.36	14.44	14.54	637.42	641.89	652.69	664.48
Blast furnaces and basic steel products	16.56	17.09	17.15	17.24	738.58	772.47	780.33	794.76
Fabricated metal products	11.91	11.92	12.04	12.08	518.09	513.75	524.94	532.73
Industrial machinery and equipment	12.99	13.02	13.10	13.16	576.76	568.97	576.40	589.57
Electronic and other electrical equipment	11.52	11.52	11.54	11.60	495.36	487.30	491.60	503.44
Transportation equipment	16.42	16.53	16.62	16.92	737.26	735.59	748.24	778.32
Motor vehicles and equipment	16.88	16.96	17.08	17.42	786.61	778.46	794.22	823.97
Instruments and related products	12.46	12.54	12.54	12.66	524.57	522.92	527.93	540.58
Miscellaneous manufacturing	9.58	9.71	9.76	9.91	388.95	394.23	397.23	400.36
Nondurable goods	11.16	11.30	11.35	11.44	459.79	466.69	471.03	477.05
Food and kindred products	10.63	10.66	10.81	10.88	439.02	446.65	456.18	458.05
Tobacco products	16.55	18.36	19.09	18.66	618.97	767.45	759.78	772.52
Textile mill products	9.01	9.20	9.26	9.28	380.22	386.40	387.99	392.54
Apparel and other textile products	7.24	7.43	7.45	7.47	272.22	282.34	283.10	285.35
Paper and allied products	13.61	13.89	13.92	13.95	605.85	615.33	616.66	620.78
Printing and publishing	12.11	12.23	12.20	12.32	471.08	475.75	477.02	482.94
Chemicals and allied products	15.08	15.35	15.34	15.44	662.84	666.19	671.89	679.36
Petroleum and coal products	18.71	19.35	19.31	19.43	812.01	872.69	865.09	870.46
Rubber and misc. plastics products	10.67	10.66	10.69	10.81	454.54	450.92	455.39	465.91
Leather and leather products	7.86	8.02	8.03	8.04	306.54	313.58	312.37	311.15
Transportation and public utilities	13.74	14.03	14.07	14.15	546.85	564.01	559.99	566.00
Wholesale trade	11.85	12.15	12.11	12.15	453.86	470.21	465.02	466.56
Retail trade	7.36	7.57	7.56	7.57	215.65	220.29	216.97	221.04
Finance, insurance, and real estate	11.65	12.02	11.97	12.02	415.91	435.12	426.13	429.11
Services	10.98	11.22	11.24	11.31	355.75	368.02	364.18	367.58

[1] See footnote 1, table B-2.

p = preliminary.

Table B-4. Average hourly earnings of production or nonsupervisory workers[1] on private nonfarm payrolls by industry, seasonally adjusted

Industry	Dec. 1993	Aug. 1994	Sept. 1994	Oct. 1994	Nov. 1994p	Dec. 1994p	Percent change from: Nov. 1994-Dec. 1994
Total private:							
Current dollars	$10.98	$11.13	$11.17	$11.25	$11.23	$11.26	0.3
Constant (1982) dollars[2]	7.40	7.36	7.38	7.43	7.39	N.A.	(3)
Mining	14.68	14.82	14.94	15.06	15.03	15.03	0
Construction	14.41	14.72	14.82	14.91	14.81	14.74	-.5
Manufacturing	11.93	12.08	12.12	12.14	12.17	12.21	.3
Excluding overtime[4]	11.32	11.43	11.46	11.51	11.48	11.60	1.0
Transportation and public utilities	13.73	13.87	13.89	14.03	14.07	14.12	.4
Wholesale trade	11.82	12.01	12.04	12.19	12.11	12.13	.2
Retail trade	7.37	7.50	7.52	7.56	7.55	7.59	.5
Finance, insurance, and real estate	11.81	11.80	11.89	12.06	11.98	11.97	-.1
Services	10.89	11.08	11.12	11.22	11.18	11.22	.4

[1] See footnote 1, table B-2.

[2] The Consumer Price Index for Urban Wage Earners and Clerical Workers (CPI-W) is used to deflate this series.

[3] Change was -.5 percent from October 1994 to November 1994, the latest month available.

[4] Derived by assuming that overtime hours are paid at the rate of time and one-half.

N.A. = not available.

p = preliminary.

 ESTABLISHMENT DATA

Table B-6. Indexes of aggregate weekly hours of production or nonsupervisory workers[1] on private nonfarm payrolls by industry

(1982=100)

Industry	Not seasonally adjusted				Seasonally adjusted					
	Dec. 1993	Oct. 1994	Nov. 1994[p]	Dec. 1994[p]	Dec. 1993	Aug. 1994	Sept. 1994	Oct. 1994	Nov. 1994[p]	Dec. 1994[p]
Total private	127.3	132.4	131.5	132.5	125.9	128.9	129.7	131.1	130.7	131.1
Goods-producing industries	105.8	111.7	111.0	110.6	105.1	107.8	108.3	108.5	109.3	110.1
Mining	56.0	56.4	56.6	55.0	55.1	55.2	55.7	55.3	55.2	54.3
Construction	124.4	147.1	140.9	134.2	128.8	134.2	136.0	134.7	137.8	139.8
Manufacturing	105.1	107.7	108.2	109.3	103.3	105.7	105.8	106.4	106.9	107.6
Durable goods	103.7	108.5	107.6	109.4	101.6	104.7	104.9	105.6	106.4	107.2
Lumber and wood products	129.0	135.7	134.1	134.4	128.7	132.0	131.0	133.3	133.2	134.3
Furniture and fixtures	126.8	128.9	128.6	130.2	122.6	125.1	126.0	126.3	126.7	126.1
Stone, clay, and glass products	102.7	112.0	110.6	108.3	104.2	107.6	107.8	108.1	108.6	110.2
Primary metal industries	87.9	91.2	92.8	94.3	86.8	89.8	90.7	91.6	92.5	93.2
Blast furnaces and basic steel products	72.5	72.6	73.3	74.5	71.7	71.5	72.4	72.9	73.5	73.4
Fabricated metal products	107.8	111.8	113.4	115.4	104.8	109.1	109.6	110.0	111.7	112.6
Industrial machinery and equipment	96.3	98.3	99.4	102.0	93.7	97.3	98.4	98.8	99.5	99.3
Electronic and other electrical equipment	104.7	106.2	108.2	111.1	101.6	105.5	105.3	106.0	106.3	107.9
Transportation equipment	115.5	117.7	120.0	124.0	112.9	116.3	116.2	117.2	119.1	120.9
Motor vehicles and equipment	148.2	156.1	159.8	164.9	145.2	153.5	154.1	155.4	159.5	160.8
Instruments and related products	76.9	73.9	74.6	75.7	75.0	74.2	74.0	73.8	74.0	74.0
Miscellaneous manufacturing	101.6	106.2	106.1	102.9	100.6	102.1	101.0	102.0	102.1	101.9
Nondurable goods	107.1	109.3	109.1	109.3	105.8	107.0	107.0	107.5	107.5	108.0
Food and kindred products	112.6	118.7	117.4	115.3	112.3	113.6	113.3	113.4	114.6	115.1
Tobacco products	63.5	66.9	60.0	65.4	56.8	60.0	59.9	60.0	57.0	58.9
Textile mill products	99.8	99.8	99.7	100.4	99.0	98.3	97.8	99.1	98.5	99.4
Apparel and other textile products	88.5	90.1	89.2	88.4	87.4	88.5	88.3	88.6	87.4	87.8
Paper and allied products	112.2	112.1	112.4	113.1	110.2	111.4	110.4	111.4	111.5	111.0
Printing and publishing	126.1	126.4	127.5	129.3	123.2	125.3	125.8	126.1	125.8	126.2
Chemicals and allied products	103.5	101.6	102.3	103.9	101.6	100.6	100.9	102.0	102.0	102.4
Petroleum and coal products	77.5	84.4	82.3	79.7	79.9	81.0	84.0	82.4	81.0	82.7
Rubber and misc. plastics products	135.9	142.1	143.2	145.2	134.1	139.5	140.8	141.0	141.6	143.4
Leather and leather products	55.7	54.6	54.1	53.7	55.0	54.0	53.6	53.5	53.4	52.8
Service-producing industries	137.0	141.7	140.7	142.3	135.2	138.3	139.4	141.2	140.2	140.6
Transportation and public utilities	119.2	122.0	121.2	122.3	117.6	118.8	119.8	120.5	119.8	120.9
Wholesale trade	113.1	117.6	116.5	116.5	112.6	114.7	115.2	116.6	116.2	115.8
Retail trade	130.2	129.3	129.9	134.5	124.1	127.6	127.5	129.7	128.8	128.6
Finance, insurance, and real estate	121.3	123.1	120.8	121.5	121.3	120.4	120.9	123.8	121.8	121.4
Services	158.8	168.6	166.7	167.1	158.9	163.8	165.9	167.9	166.7	167.8

[1] See footnote 1, table B-2.

p = preliminary.

 ESTABLISHMENT DATA

Table B-6. Diffusion indexes of employment change, seasonally adjusted

(Percent)

Time span	Jan.	Feb.	Mar.	Apr.	May	June	July	Aug.	Sept.	Oct.	Nov.	Dec.
	Private nonfarm payrolls, 356 industries[1]											
Over 1-month span:												
1990	58.8	57.3	50.8	47.9	49.7	51.8	43.8	46.2	42.7	41.6	41.3	41.3
1991	39.6	39.6	38.5	38.2	48.5	45.4	48.3	52.0	48.9	46.8	46.5	46.1
1992	42.1	46.1	48.3	57.7	53.1	50.4	52.8	46.5	53.4	56.9	52.5	57.3
1993	57.9	61.7	49.0	56.0	57.0	51.1	58.8	50.0	56.7	57.4	61.0	57.4
1994	56.6	58.3	62.9	62.5	56.3	63.2	59.3	59.8	56.9	59.8	p63.5	p61.2
Over 3-month span:												
1990	59.0	59.1	52.5	48.9	49.0	47.3	45.9	40.6	38.3	38.2	35.7	35.4
1991	34.3	32.0	31.6	38.2	39.3	44.2	49.4	50.7	50.8	44.9	43.7	40.9
1992	39.7	42.3	51.0	56.2	57.6	54.1	50.4	49.9	51.7	56.2	58.6	59.8
1993	64.0	61.4	59.7	55.8	54.9	57.7	54.6	55.9	55.8	62.4	61.5	60.8
1994	62.1	64.6	65.2	65.0	65.4	64.6	66.7	64.0	65.4	p65.6	p68.5	
Over 6-month span:												
1990	57.2	54.9	55.8	50.4	46.8	44.0	41.3	38.9	35.8	33.6	32.0	30.2
1991	30.2	32.4	31.2	33.7	39.2	44.7	46.5	45.6	47.8	44.6	41.4	39.9
1992	43.5	46.3	47.2	52.0	54.2	56.6	52.8	53.1	55.8	56.3	64.2	62.2
1993	61.4	60.8	59.0	59.8	54.4	54.5	57.9	58.8	59.7	60.8	62.8	63.6
1994	67.0	65.9	68.8	66.0	67.8	66.3	68.1	p70.5	p67.7			
Over 12-month span:												
1990	55.5	52.7	51.7	48.5	45.4	42.6	39.3	36.1	35.8	33.0	33.0	30.6
1991	31.0	31.0	31.7	31.9	31.7	33.8	35.8	37.5	40.0	45.2	45.6	45.4
1992	47.2	42.3	42.7	44.1	48.0	52.5	55.8	60.7	59.7	60.4	60.1	60.7
1993	60.9	61.1	60.7	62.2	63.2	62.1	62.4	60.8	63.5	62.8	63.1	63.5
1994	64.2	65.7	66.0	66.4	p67.4	p69.7						
	Manufacturing payrolls, 139 industries[1]											
Over 1-month span:												
1990	48.9	47.8	43.9	46.8	40.3	46.8	38.8	42.4	35.6	38.5	29.1	34.2
1991	32.7	35.8	31.3	37.4	45.7	43.5	46.4	49.3	42.8	47.8	41.4	39.6
1992	38.1	40.8	45.0	57.9	47.8	50.0	53.2	41.7	49.3	47.8	52.5	51.8
1993	52.5	57.8	47.8	41.7	46.0	40.3	49.3	42.8	46.8	50.0	55.4	51.1
1994	54.3	63.8	61.1	66.1	50.0	58.6	52.9	56.8	48.9	60.8	p60.4	p60.1
Over 3-month span:												
1990	44.6	45.3	45.0	38.8	41.7	38.8	38.1	28.8	30.9	23.0	23.0	21.6
1991	24.5	21.9	20.5	32.7	36.3	39.6	47.1	46.0	48.2	39.9	36.7	33.5
1992	30.9	36.3	45.3	50.7	55.4	53.6	47.1	47.1	42.4	50.0	51.1	55.0
1993	60.1	58.3	51.4	40.6	37.1	43.5	40.3	41.0	43.2	52.9	54.7	56.1
1994	56.1	57.8	56.5	53.2	57.2	55.8	61.5	55.0	60.4	p60.1	p67.8	
Over 6-month span:												
1990	43.5	39.9	42.8	41.0	36.3	34.2	29.1	25.2	22.3	21.2	18.0	16.9
1991	15.8	20.9	21.2	26.3	34.9	39.2	42.1	40.3	40.3	37.1	32.4	32.7
1992	34.2	37.1	41.0	48.6	52.2	54.7	46.4	49.3	50.4	48.9	57.9	56.8
1993	54.0	51.8	48.6	47.1	37.1	34.2	39.6	45.7	47.8	50.4	54.3	55.8
1994	58.3	56.1	59.4	54.3	58.3	56.8	60.1	p63.3	p61.9			
Over 12-month span:												
1990	37.8	35.3	33.5	33.1	28.1	26.3	23.7	20.5	19.4	16.5	16.2	15.8
1991	16.5	16.2	17.3	18.0	20.9	24.1	26.3	30.6	32.7	38.1	38.8	37.4
1992	42.4	38.7	36.3	36.0	39.6	45.7	50.0	55.8	57.9	55.4	52.9	52.9
1993	50.0	52.5	48.6	49.3	50.7	48.9	50.0	48.9	50.0	50.7	51.4	51.4
1994	50.7	54.3	54.0	56.8	p58.3	p61.9						

[1] Based on seasonally adjusted data for 1-, 3-, and 6-month spans and unadjusted data for the 12-month span. Data are centered within the span.

p = preliminary.

NOTE: Figures are the percent of industries with employment increasing plus one-half of the industries with unchanged employment, where 50 percent indicates an equal balance between industries with increasing and decreasing employment.

COMPARISON OF UNEMPLOYMENT INSURANCE DATA TO CPS TOTAL UNEMPLOYMENT
(Numbers in thousands, not seasonally adjusted)

January 5, 1995

WEEK ENDING DATE	UI PROGRAMS - CONTINUED CLAIMS: REGULAR UI PROGRAM STATE UI	UCFE	UCX	REGULAR EXTENDED BENEFITS 1/	FEDERAL EXTENDED BENEFITS 2/	TOTAL (INCL. RRB) 3/	CPS TOTAL UNEMPLOYMENT	REGULAR UI AS PERCENT OF CPS TOTAL UNEMPLOYED	REGULAR UI AS PERCENT OF CPS JOB LOSERS	TOTAL UI AS PERCENT OF CPS TOTAL UNEMPLOYED	TOTAL UI AS PERCENT OF CPS JOB LOSERS
Historical Data											
05/17/75	4,338.8	40.9	93.3	760.4	691.5	5,942.9	7,715.0	58.0	100.9	77.0	134.1
05/12/79	2,079.6	24.8	45.4	69.2	0.0	2,232.0	5,419.0	39.7	99.0	41.2	102.8
07/12/80	3,757.4	28.8	64.7	278.5	0.0	4,162.4	8,603.0	44.8	86.5	48.4	93.8
04/18/81	2,923.9	31.3	46.4	337.8	0.0	3,380.3	7,561.0	39.7	74.8	44.7	84.0
Annual Averages 4/											
1980	3,389.9	29.5	55.2	346.3	0.0	3,802.9	7,637.0	45.5	88.0	50.0	96.8
1981	3,061.9	32.0	40.7	231.1	0.0	3,365.7	8,273.0	37.9	73.5	40.7	78.9
1982	4,041.0	31.9	43.1	402.4	0.0	4,518.4	10,678.0	38.5	65.7	42.3	72.1
1983	3,402.3	26.2	29.1	255.7	854.0	4,567.3	8,992.0	38.5	55.3	50.8	73.0
1984	2,399.4	23.2	20.7	4.3	381.5	2,837.8	8,539.0	28.6	55.2	33.2	64.2
1985	2,538.6	21.0	19.4	4.6	110.1	2,718.4	8,312.0	31.0	61.6	32.7	64.9
1986	2,579.9	23.2	19.3	18.5	0.0	2,666.4	8,237.0	31.8	65.0	32.4	66.1
1987	2,267.8	21.4	17.8	8.9	0.0	2,335.7	7,425.0	31.1	64.7	31.5	65.5
1988	2,062.3	23.4	18.7	1.0	0.0	2,119.1	6,701.0	31.4	68.1	31.6	68.5
1989	2,111.6	21.3	14.6	0.7	0.0	2,158.9	6,528.0	32.9	72.8	33.1	73.2
1990	2,474.5	23.8	18.5	1.4	0.0	2,529.0	6,874.0	36.0	75.8	36.8	76.1
1991	3,256.7	30.1	22.1	28.0	135.7	3,483.3	8,426.0	39.3	71.8	41.3	75.6
1992	3,171.3	32.2	60.8	0.2	1,527.6	4,801.0	9,384.0	34.8	61.7	51.2	90.7
1993	2,713.7	32.5	54.3	7.7	1,311.4	4,127.0	8,734.0	32.1	58.7	47.3	86.5
Current Data 5/											
07/17/93	2,683.7	30.4	51.2	0.0	1,378.1	4,148.4	9,002.0	30.7	59.4	46.1	89.2
08/14/93	2,514.0	30.4	49.3	0.0	1,355.6	3,954.3	8,470.0	30.8	56.6	46.7	86.3
09/18/93	2,274.2	31.8	47.3	0.0	1,330.1	3,688.4	8,128.0	29.0	55.9	45.4	87.7
10/16/93	2,313.3	35.9	48.3	16.5	1,180.1	3,599.1	8,101.0	29.6	56.7	44.4	85.2
11/13/93	2,491.6	37.4	47.3	30.9	935.8	3,549.0	7,890.0	32.7	61.4	45.0	84.6
12/11/93	2,776.0	40.5	47.2	44.4	1,142.8	4,058.9	7,764.0	36.9	63.8	52.3	90.4
01/15/94	3,125.1	34.9	43.3	35.8	725.0	3,973.2	9,492.0	33.7	61.4	41.9	76.2
02/12/94	3,554.0	37.3	46.1	35.9	677.0	4,360.2	9,262.0	39.3	73.9	47.1	88.5
03/12/94	3,262.2	33.7	42.3	8.4	355.8	3,712.2	8,874.0	37.6	73.8	41.8	82.1
04/16/94	2,786.1	30.3	39.1	11.9	159.1	3,033.8	8,078.0	35.3	74.5	37.6	79.2
05/14/94	2,564.9	27.5	36.6	11.2	0.0	2,645.1	7,658.0	34.3	79.2	34.5	79.7
06/18/94	2,403.6	25.6	34.1	26.8	0.0	2,494.0	8,251.0	29.9	71.2	30.2	72.1
07/16/94	2,616.5	28.7	34.7	26.2	0.0	2,709.0	8,281.0	32.4	72.4	32.7	73.2
08/13/94	2,384.8	29.3	34.8	29.6	0.0	2,486.5	7,668.0	31.1	68.7	31.6	69.7
09/17/94	2,102.4	30.6	34.7	6.0	0.0	2,179.8	7,379.0	29.4	62.1	29.5	62.4
10/15/94	2,124.8	36.6	35.5	1.5	0.0	2,203.3	7,155.0	30.7	69.3	30.8	69.5
11/12/94	2,256.5	36.4	34.6	0.7	0.0	2,332.2	6,973.0	33.4	69.1	33.4	69.3
12/10/94	2,504.3	39.6	36.1	0.5	0.0	2,586.6	6,690.0	38.6	73.4	38.7	73.6

1/ Prior to 1980, there were national and individual State "on" triggers for extended benefits; since 1980, Extended Benefits have been payable under Individual State "on" triggers only.

2/ The Federal Supplemental Compensation program was in effect from January 1982 through June 1985, but data are are only available begining in 1983.
The Emergency Unemployment Compensation Act was in effect from November 17, 1991 to February 5, 1994.

3/ Railroad Retirement Board claims are not available until 1984

4/ Unemployment insurance data for 1980 83 are not strictly comparable with data for 1984 and forward

5/ Begining in January 1994 data from the Current Population Survey reflect the redesigned survey and new population controls. The new data are not directly comparable with historical CPS data.

UI EXTENDED BENEFITS PROGRAMS

Regular State UI Extended Benefits (EB)

As of December 30, 1994, no States were triggered on under the State EB program.

A State triggers "on" for regular State extended benefits when:

IUR Required. The State 13-week IUR is at least 5 percent and is 20 percent higher than the average of the same 13 week period in the two previous years. Thirteen weeks of EB are available.

IUR Option. When the "20 percent factor" is not met, a State which has enacted the option in its law, may pay extended benefits when the State IUR reaches 6 percent regardless of the IUR in previous years. Thirteen weeks of benefits are available.

TUR Alternative. The seasonally adjusted State TUR for the most recent 3-months published is at least 6.5 percent and is 10 percent or more above the State TUR for the same 3-month period in either of the two preceding years. Thirteen weeks of benefits are available. If the 3-month seasonally adjusted TUR is 8.0 or greater and the 10 percent or more criterion is met, 20 weeks of benefits are available.

Currently, eight States have the TUR alternative trigger in law: Alaska, Connecticut, Kansas, New Jersey, Oregon, Rhode Island, Vermont, and the State of Washington. Maine no longer has this option in law.

Emergency Unemployment Compensation Act (EUCA)

The EUCA of 1991 expired February 5, 1994.

1/5/95

U.S. UNEMPLOYMENT INSURANCE EXHAUSTION DATA

EXHAUSTIONS OF REGULAR STATE UI, EXTENDED BENEFITS,
AND TEMPORARY FEDERAL EXTENDED BENEFITS
(IN THOUSANDS)

HISTORIAL DATA: MONTHLY AVERAGE

YEAR	STATE REGULAR UI	STATE REGULAR UI EXHAUSTEE RATE
1975	350	37.8
1976	273	37.8
1977	237	33.4
1978	169	26.8
1979	170	26.8
1980	256	33.2
1981	249	32.4
1982	346	38.5
1983	349	38.4
1984	219	34.3
1985	213	31.1
1986	225	32.5
1987	202	30.8
1988	165	28.5
1989	163	28.0
1990	193	29.4
1991	289	34.8
1992	304	39.7
1993	267	39.2

MONTHLY DATA

MONTH	YEAR	STATE REGULAR UI	STATE EXTENDED BENEFITS	FEDERAL EXTENDED BENEFITS	STATE REG UI EXH RATE
1	1989	169.0	0	0	30.3
2		151.6	0	0	30.1
3		178.7	0	0	30.0
4		163.8	0	0	36.5
5		172.5	1	0	29.6
6		149.3	0	0	29.6
7		159.6	0	0	28.9
8		172.6	0	0	29.2
9		148.3	0	0	28.9
10		151.6	0	0	28.9
11		156.3	0	0	28.5
12		150.9	0	0	28.5
1	1990	202.8	0	0	28.7
2		168.8	0	0	28.2
3		190.9	0	0	27.9
4		195.3	0	0	27.5
5		207.9	0	0	27.3
6		184.0	0	0	27.4
7		207.2	0	0	27.4
8		201.8	0	0	27.0
9		168.7	0	0	27.8
10		197.8	0	0	27.8
11		191.3	0	0	27.9
12		204.7	0	0	28.0
1	1991	265.3	0	0	28.4
2		228.4	0	0	28.2
3		261.3	0	0	28.1
4		306.2	3	0	28.2
5		315.0	0	0	28.3
6		277.9	24	0	28.4
7		349.7	15	0	28.1
8		318.5	5	0	28.2
9		275.7	1	0	28.4
10		303.0	2	0	28.6
11		262.2	1	0	28.8
12		314.2	0	1	29.4

MONTHLY DATA

MONTH	YEAR	STATE REGULAR UI	STATE EXTENDED BENEFITS	FEDERAL EXTENDED BENEFITS	STATE REG UI EXH RATE
1	1992	359.5	0	23	29.9
2		302.8	0	28	30.5
3		342.9	1	29	31.1
4		363.7	1	58	32.0
5		324.2	6	171	32.5
6		335.4	4	119	32.8
7		358.2	4	335	33.1
8		312.1	1	138	33.2
9		295.5	0	148	33.5
10		278.0	0	146	33.8
11		256.0	0	170	34.0
12		305.8	0	245	34.8
1	1993	292.9	0	242	35.4
2		265.1	0	188	36.0
3		304.7	0	211	36.7
4		288.9	0	188	37.2
5		249.5	0	183	37.7
6		269.1	0	200	37.6
7		270.0	0	183	38.6
8		268.2	0	193	39.2
9		252.5	0	185	39.1
10		236.7	0	160	39.2
11		244.8	0	217	39.5
12		261.6	0	330	39.3
1	1994	270.5	18	324	39.8
2		239.8	12	236	40.0
3		281.8	5	217	40.1
4		268.3	5	99	40.0
5		264.7	5	23	39.8
6		260.8	6	1	39.6
7		251.7 r	6	1	38.8
8		281.9 r	15	1	38.0
9		216.8 r	4	1	37.6
10		215.1 r	4	1	37.5
11		228.3 p	4 p	1 p	36.9
12					

Exhaustions - the number of beneficiaries of UI programs who use up their maximum benefit award in a benefit year. Exhaustions represent the total number of final payments in a period.

Regular UI - unemployment insurance benefits for workers covered by State UI law

Extended Benefits - Permanent State UI program that provides additional benefit payments beyond regular benefits, and is triggered by high unemployment in each state.

Federal Extended Benefits - Nationally funded UI programs which provide additional benefits on a temporary basis, and are triggered by high unemployment in each state.

State Regular UI Exhaustion Rate - the proportion of eligible beneficiaries who use up the maximum amount of benefits in a benefit year. The rate is calculated by dividing the most recent 12-month average of final payments by the 12-month average of first payments ending six months previous.

Note: Data include Puerto Rico

January 5, 1994